There Is Room For More

Building Capacity at Every Level

Dr. Joke Solanke
Atlanta, Georgia, USA

Purpose and Pathway Publications

First Edition

Published by Purpose and Pathway Publications Atlanta, Georgia, USA
www.purposeandpathwaypublications.com

Disclaimer

This book is intended for educational and informational purposes only. While the author draws from leadership experience, historical examples, and observational insight, this work does not constitute legal, financial, medical, or professional advice. Readers are encouraged to exercise discernment and seek appropriate professional counsel where necessary.

The views expressed are those of the author and are presented to encourage reflection, growth, and responsible leadership development.

Scripture & Conceptual References

Biblical principles referenced in this book are used for conceptual and illustrative purposes only and are not intended as theological instruction. Scriptural narratives may be paraphrased or selectively cited to support leadership and capacity-building insights unless otherwise noted.

ISBN

Paperback ISBN: 978-1-968717-09-4

eBook ISBN: 978-1-968717-10-0

Design & Formatting

Interior design and formatting by Purpose and Pathway Publications

Printed in the United States of America

To God Almighty, whose breath gave me life and whose wisdom orders my steps. My existence is anchored in Your love, and my capacity is formed by YOUR HAND.

I am eternally grateful for the grace to carry what You entrust to me.

Acknowledgements

This work was not built in isolation.

I gratefully acknowledge the Divine Perspectives audience, the viewers who consistently showed up, listened, reflected, and returned. Through weekly broadcast teaching, it became evident where clarity was needed, where gaps existed, and where understanding of capacity required deeper articulation. This book emerged not from questioning, but from observation, discernment, and sustained engagement with those receiving the teaching.

I also acknowledge the teams who labor with me through Blossom Life Outreach, those who carry vision, steward responsibility, and execute with excellence across conferences, gatherings, and collaborative assignments. Your consistency and commitment have shaped both this work and my understanding of capacity in practice.

I honor the mentors and guides, past and present, whose insight, challenge, and example refined my thinking and stretched my leadership. I acknowledge the mentees who entrusted me with their growth and, in doing so, sharpened my clarity and conviction.

To my family, whose presence, patience, and grounding influence have sustained me through seasons of building, thank you.

And to every encounter, direct or indirect, that influenced a decision, exposed a gap, or demanded recalibration, this work carries the imprint of those moments.

Capacity is never built alone. It is revealed through stewardship, refined through responsibility, and sustained by grace

TABLE OF CONTENTS

Those who accomplished extraordinary things in the past did not arrive fully formed. They built capacity deliberately, step by step, often in obscurity long before their impact became visible.

Dr. Joke Solanke

INTRODUCTION

◆————————————◆

Why Capacity, Not Opportunity, Determines Outcomes

———

Why Capacity Determines Outcomes

The end of the year often places us in a posture of reflection, assessment, reassessment, and evaluation of the journey behind us. For me, this reflective season feels like having multiple browser windows open at once, active, intentional, and alive with possibility.

As I began outlining plans for the new year, I found myself revisiting past conversations from *Divine Perspectives*, a weekly broadcast I host on YouTube. While listening, one playlist arrested my attention, a series of teachings on capacity building delivered earlier in the year.

What began as a casual review became something else entirely.

As I listened, I became a student of my own teaching. Ideas I had shared instinctively with others returned with unusual clarity and weight. I was not emotionally stirred; I was intellectually awakened. In that moment, the writer in me surfaced, insisting that what had been taught verbally needed to be extracted, refined, and preserved.

It became clear that these teachings were not confined to spiritual formation or personal development. They applied seamlessly to leadership, governance, healthcare systems, institutions, families, communities, and even nations.

What I had taught as spiritual insight revealed itself as leadership architecture.

The Unseen Difference Between Overflow and Overwhelm

One of the central narratives referenced throughout the original teaching series is the story of a woman in financial crisis following her husband's death, a crisis intensified by ignorance, mismanagement, and debt. What neither she nor those around her initially recognized was the value of what already existed in her possession.

The oil she carried held no value to her, not because it was insignificant, but because she lacked the understanding required to steward it. She did not yet understand how capacity is built, often through collaboration, structure, and alignment with others. Life is designed in such a way that no individual holds custody of everything required for greatness. What we lack is often supplied through connection, instruction, and shared function.

This story reveals a deeper truth. If we are not taught how things work, we will never know how to work them. Resources without understanding remain dormant. Potential without structure stays unexpressed.

Capacity, therefore, does not mean possessing more than what one has in the present moment. It means developing the ability to steward what already exists, to recognize its value, and to engage the systems and relationships necessary for it to multiply.

What changed the woman's situation was not the sudden appearance of something new, but the revelation of how to work with what she already had.

In reflecting on that story, I made a statement that later became foundational to this book:

"That woman got to overflow not because of the oil, but because she built capacity."

This single sentence reframes how outcomes are commonly understood.

Most people attribute success to visible factors such as talent, education, connections, funding, timing, or favor. While these elements matter, they are not predictive. They explain access, not sustainability.

Capacity, however, predicts outcomes with unsettling accuracy.

Capacity is the unseen infrastructure that determines whether opportunity produces overflow or overwhelm.

It answers questions many leaders never pause to ask. Can this responsibility be sustained? Can this growth be governed? Can this pressure be absorbed without collapse?

Across every sphere of life, the principle holds true.

Outcomes never exceed the capacity built to contain them.

Capacity Is Not Personal Alone

In another moment from the same teaching series, I observed:

"The resources, the relationships, the conversations that we need to get to overflow, we release them today."

Embedded in this statement is a critical leadership truth. Capacity is not merely personal. It is relational, structural, and systemic.

Capacity includes people, processes, discernment, conversations, timing, and governance. It is not inherited automatically through talent or access. It is built deliberately, often quietly, long before outcomes become visible.

This explains why some individuals with extraordinary talent fail, while others with modest beginnings thrive. Why some with powerful connections collapse under pressure, while others sustain influence without spectacle.

The Myth That Growth Fixes Weakness

One of the most persistent myths in leadership is the belief that growth will resolve internal weaknesses. In reality, growth magnifies them.

Expansion does not heal gaps; it exposes them. Promotion does not correct immaturity; it reveals it. Influence does not strengthen structure; it tests it.

This is why individuals and institutions often collapse not in obscurity, but at the height of opportunity.

Stamina: The Missing Conversation

Another dimension that surfaced repeatedly throughout the capacity-building series was stamina. In one session, I spoke about the need for:

"Spiritual stamina, physical stamina, emotional stamina, mental stamina, leadership stamina, and financial discipline to carry the weight."

Stamina is rarely discussed in leadership literature, yet it is one of the most decisive factors in longevity. Vision without stamina burns out. Authority without emotional regulation becomes destructive. Resources without discipline create instability.

Capacity, therefore, is not about doing more. It is about being built to carry more, without breaking.

Why This Book Exists

This book was written to move the conversation beyond surface-level inspiration and to explore capacity with greater depth and intention. It is not designed to stir emotion for a moment, but to engage understanding over time. Its purpose is to examine the internal and external structures that determine whether responsibility, influence, and outcomes can be sustained across seasons of growth.

At the heart of this work is a simple but often overlooked truth. There is always room for more, regardless of one's current level.

Growth is not reserved for beginners, nor does it end with achievement. Every level reached introduces the demands of the next, and capacity must expand accordingly.

As this teaching developed, I came to a personal realization that reshaped its depth and direction. I needed, and will continue to need, the very principles explored in these pages. That discovery revealed the universality and agelessness of capacity. These principles are not bound to age, profession, or era. They govern progress itself.

Those who accomplished extraordinary things in the past did not arrive fully formed. They built capacity deliberately, step by step, often in obscurity long before their impact became visible. The same pattern holds true today. Meaningful and lasting results are sustained only when internal and external capacity grows alongside opportunity.

This pattern is evident across every field. Influence changes hands not merely because opportunities shift, but because capacity must keep pace with expansion. When growth outpaces capacity, instability follows. When capacity is developed intentionally, endurance becomes possible.

This book, therefore, is not merely descriptive. It is directional. It provides a guide and a path for identifying where capacity is required, how it is built, and why neglecting it eventually limits progress.

The principles in these pages are not mere observations, nor are they ideological assertions. They are drawn from Scripture, reinforced by lived experience, and proven through consistent application. They explain why some leaders endure, why certain organizations stabilize while others fragment, and why outcomes can often be discerned long before results appear.

As I reminded listeners toward the close of that original teaching series:

Dr. Joke Solanke

"We will not get overwhelmed. We will go line by line, precept upon precept, and celebrate every little progress until we get to overflow."

Capacity is not built in leaps. It is built incrementally, intentionally, and with restraint. The goal is not speed, visibility, or applause. The goal is sustainability, preservation, and legacy.

A Final Invitation

If you have ever wondered why opportunity feels heavier than expected, why progress brings pressure instead of peace, or why success feels fragile despite effort, this book offers a different lens.

Sometimes opportunities are not delayed because there is no more available, but because the capacity for more has not yet been built.

This book exists to help fill that gap.

Join me as we build capacity for our lives, our communities, our institutions, and the futures we hope to sustain

Capacity is not built by becoming something else. It is built by becoming excellent at what you are, while learning how to collaborate with what you are not.

Dr. Joke Solanke

CHAPTER 1

◆——————————————◆

Identity, Foundation, and the Limits of Skill

——

Y ou cannot build capacity without first knowing what you are designed to carry.

She was competent. Experienced. Tenured. Highly skilled.

If leadership were defined solely by execution, by getting things done, she excelled.

She understood workflows intimately. She followed protocols with precision. She met deadlines consistently and delivered outcomes with a reliability that made her indispensable. When problems arose, she was often the one called upon to fix them. When systems stalled, she was the one who kept things moving.

Her supervisors trusted her judgment. Her peers respected her efficiency. In meetings, her input carried weight because it was practical, grounded, and proven. She was not theoretical. She was effective.

Yet she was stuck.

Not visibly stuck. There was no failure to point to, no reprimand on record, no dramatic breakdown. But her growth had slowed, and she could feel it. Opportunities seemed to circulate around her without fully opening. Conversations about advancement never quite materialized into movement. The momentum she once enjoyed had leveled off.

She assumed, as many high performers do, that advancement was primarily a function of competence. If she kept improving her skills, the next level would open. That belief shaped her entire development strategy.

She enrolled in additional trainings. She accumulated certifications. She sharpened her technical mastery. She became even better at what she already did well.

From the outside, her résumé looked impressive. From the inside, something felt increasingly misaligned.

What she never paused to examine was something far more consequential.

She did not stop to evaluate where she truly was, what she already carried, what the next level would demand, what it would cost her to remain there, or what she would need to outgrow that level as well.

Her preparation was technical, not architectural.

She was strengthening execution without examining structure. She was refining skill without assessing capacity. She was preparing to do more without considering whether she could carry more.

When she eventually approached me for a recommendation to interview for a leadership development program, one that could open the door for her to become a facility administrator, I immediately recognized the gap. I had walked that path before. I understood the difference between doing work and governing systems.

Technically, she was ready. Structurally and emotionally, she was not.

The interview would not disqualify her on skill. It would expose something more fundamental. It would confront her on capacity.

When Skill Stops Being the Differentiator

At entry and mid-level positions, skill is currency. Competence distinguishes one candidate from another. Efficiency is rewarded. Productivity is visible and measurable. Those who execute reliably are promoted, trusted, and relied upon.

But as leadership responsibility increases, the rules change.

At higher levels of leadership, competence is assumed. Everyone in the room knows how to execute. Everyone understands processes. Everyone has experience. Skill becomes baseline rather than differentiator.

What distinguishes leaders at that level is not what they can do, but what they can carry.

The next level she desired was not a doing role. It was a bearing role.

At that level, you are blamed for failures you did not personally commit. You are accountable for systems you did not personally design. You absorb pressure generated by other people's decisions. You manage dissatisfaction, conflict, and ambiguity without losing clarity. You are responsible for outcomes even when resources are limited. You make decisions that disappoint some people permanently.

This is the point at which leadership stops being transactional and becomes structural.

Many skilled professionals stall here, not because they lack intelligence or work ethic, but because they have not built the mental, emotional, relational, and structural capacity required for that responsibility.

Did she have potential? Absolutely. Were opportunities available? Yes. Was she willing to stretch beyond her comfort zone? No.

Capacity exposes willingness long before it rewards ability.

Before Capacity, Identity Must Be Clear

Before capacity can be defined or built, identity must be clarified.

Without identity, capacity becomes a misguided pursuit. People attempt to build what they were never designed to carry. They compete where collaboration is required. They interpret limitation as failure rather than design.

Identity answers the foundational question. What am I created to be responsible for?

Capacity answers a different one. How much can I carry within that responsibility?

When these questions are confused, growth becomes exhausting instead of empowering. People chase expansion without alignment. They measure themselves against roles they were never meant to inhabit. Over time, effort increases while fulfillment decreases.

One of the most damaging assumptions in leadership culture is the belief that growth requires becoming everything.

It does not. Growth requires becoming clear.

Limitation Is Not Deficiency

Limitation is often treated as something to overcome, hide, or apologize for. In reality, limitation is one of the most precise indicators of design.

Limitation is not deficiency. Deficiency is absence. Limitation is structure.

If I am the hand by identity, I cannot build capacity to think. That is not failure. It is precision. The hand is not defective because it does not reason or analyze. Its strength lies in execution, movement, grip, and coordination.

Trying to force the hand to become the brain does not increase capacity. It creates frustration, inefficiency, and eventual burnout.

Capacity is not built by becoming something else. It is built by becoming excellent at what you are, while learning how to collaborate with what you are not.

This distinction is critical.

Many leaders exhaust themselves trying to compensate for design through effort. They over-function in areas that should be supported externally. They mistake exhaustion for sacrifice and misalignment for commitment.

Identity removes shame from limitation and replaces it with wisdom.

Identity Sets the Boundaries for Capacity

Identity establishes the boundaries within which capacity can grow. It clarifies what should be strengthened, what should be supported, what should be delegated, and what requires partnership rather than personal mastery.

The hand does not compete with the brain. It collaborates with it. Together, they achieve what neither could alone.

Leaders who misunderstand identity attempt to carry everything personally. They centralize responsibility unnecessarily. Over time, effort becomes unsustainable, and collapse is reframed as burnout rather than misalignment.

Understanding identity is not about narrowing ambition. It is about aligning ambition with design.

Foundation Precedes Height

Capacity does not exist in isolation. It rests on prerequisites.

Every structure carries a silent truth. Its height is determined not by ambition, but by foundation.

The foundation is invisible once the building stands, yet it governs everything the structure can become. It determines how much weight can be carried, how much pressure can be absorbed, and how much expansion is possible without collapse.

I recall a story from Ibadan, Nigeria, that illustrates this with sobering clarity.

A man laid the foundation for a single-storey building. Midway through construction, he changed his mind. He decided to build three storeys instead. Without reinforcing the foundation, he continued upward.

Before the roofing stage, cracks appeared. Walls began to split. The structure moved toward collapse.

The issue was not workmanship. It was not inferior materials. It was not lack of effort.

It was a capacity mismatch.

A foundation designed for one level cannot suddenly carry three.

This is not merely a construction principle. It is a leadership law.

Capacity Is About What Can Be Sustained

Many people confuse ambition with capacity. They assume desire authorizes demand. It does not.

Capacity answers a sobering question. What can be sustained without breaking, over time?

You can attempt many things without capacity. You can enter rooms you are not built to govern. You can receive opportunities you are not structured to sustain.

But outcomes eventually reveal the truth.

This is why people with extraordinary talent sometimes fail publicly, while others with modest beginnings thrive quietly. Why promotions become burdens, influence becomes pressure, and success becomes fragile.

Capacity is not revealed when things go well. It is revealed when weight is applied.

The Hidden Cost of Skipping Assessment

One of the most dangerous habits in leadership development is skipping assessment.

Many people move from one level to the next without pausing to ask. What am I currently carrying? Where am I already stretched? What am I compensating for with effort? What systems are missing? What weaknesses have I normalized?

Without assessment, growth becomes accidental. Leaders rely on adrenaline, urgency, and goodwill to bridge gaps that should be addressed structurally.

This approach works temporarily. It is not sustainable.

The woman who approached me had invested heavily in skills, but not in self-awareness, emotional regulation, or systemic thinking. The next level would require her to govern people and systems, not merely execute tasks.

Capacity gaps do not disqualify leaders. Unacknowledged capacity gaps do.

What Capacity Is Not

Before capacity can be defined accurately, it must first be distinguished from what it is not. Many leadership failures do not occur because capacity is absent, but because it is misidentified.

Capacity is often confused with visible strengths. These strengths can open doors, attract attention, and create opportunity, but they do not determine sustainability.

They explain access. They do not explain endurance.

To understand capacity correctly, we must separate it from the qualities most often mistaken for it.

Capacity is not talent
Capacity is not intelligence
Capacity is not charisma
Capacity is not experience
Capacity is not opportunity
Capacity is not visibility
Capacity is not ambition

These may grant access, but they do not guarantee sustainability.

Capacity is not how much you can do in a moment. It is how much you can carry consistently without collapse.

Readiness Before Definition

Capacity-building begins with readiness, not desire.

Readiness is not eagerness. It is not hunger for recognition. It is not impatience for promotion.

Readiness involves willingness to be uncomfortable, openness to evaluation, acceptance of accountability, humility to redesign oneself, and patience to build before expanding.

Many people want the next level. Fewer are willing to become the kind of person that level requires.

Why This Matters Now

We live in a time of accelerated opportunity. Doors open faster than structures are built. Visibility expands before maturity stabilizes. Access arrives before governance is established.

This environment rewards movement but punishes fragility.

Capacity is what protects leaders from being crushed by the very opportunities they prayed for.

The Journey Ahead

This book is not about achieving more. It is about becoming built.

In the chapters ahead, we will define capacity clearly, explore its dimensions, expose common failure patterns, and outline how capacity can be built deliberately across individuals, institutions, systems, families, and nations.

But we begin here, with identity and foundation.

Because no matter how high you aspire to build, the structure will only rise to the level the foundation can support.

Most people do not fail because they lacked vision, intelligence, or opportunity. They fail because they exceeded their capacity without recognizing it.

CHAPTER 2

◆ ———————————————— ◆

What Capacity Really Is

—

C apacity is the unseen infrastructure beneath visible success.
Capacity is one of the most frequently referenced and least understood concepts in leadership, growth, and human development. It is often used loosely to explain failure, justify delay, or rationalize limitation, yet rarely defined with the clarity required to make it actionable.

Before capacity can be built, it must be understood. Before it can be understood, it must be distinguished from effort, performance, talent, or desire. And before it can be expanded, it must be recognized as architecture rather than aspiration.

Capacity is not an abstract idea. It is a measurable, observable structure that governs outcomes long before results appear.

What Capacity Is

Capacity is the ability to carry responsibility, pressure, complexity, and growth over time without collapse.

It is not what you can do once. It is what you can sustain repeatedly.

Capacity determines whether opportunity produces overflow or overwhelm. It explains why two people, organizations, or systems can encounter the same opportunity and experience vastly different results. One stabilizes. The other fractures.

Capacity is the unseen infrastructure beneath visible success.

Capacity Is Structural, Not Emotional

Capacity is often misunderstood as an emotional state, how someone feels about responsibility, readiness, or pressure. But capacity is not primarily emotional. It is structural.

Structure determines:

i.   How weight is distributed,

ii. How pressure is absorbed,

iii. How complexity is governed,

iv. How failure is contained,

v.   How recovery occurs.

A structure may appear strong under light pressure and still fail under sustained load. The same is true of people and institutions. Many function well during stable seasons but collapse when responsibility becomes prolonged rather than episodic.

Capacity answers a sobering question: What happens when pressure does not leave?

Capacity Explains Why Outcomes Are Predictable

One of the most uncomfortable truths about capacity is that outcomes are often predictable long before they are visible.

When leaders burn out, organizations implode, or systems fail, observers often describe the collapse as sudden. In reality, collapse is rarely sudden. It is cumulative. It occurs when sustained pressure exceeds structural limits.

Capacity explains:

i.   Why talented leaders fail publicly,

ii. Why fast-growing organizations implode internally

iii. Why promotions become burdens,

iv. Why influence becomes fragile.

Capacity failure is not mysterious. It is mathematical.

How Capacity Failure Actually Shows Up

Capacity failure is rarely announced. It does not arrive with warning signs that say "collapse ahead." Instead, it presents itself in patterns that are often misinterpreted as work ethic problems, personality flaws, or temporary seasons of pressure.

Most people do not fail because they lacked vision, intelligence, or opportunity. They fail because they exceeded their capacity without recognizing it.

Capacity failure has recognizable symptoms. When these symptoms persist, they are not circumstantial. They are structural.

Chronic Urgency

One of the clearest signs of capacity failure is chronic urgency.

Urgency becomes the operating system. Everything is immediate. Everything feels critical. There is no margin, no pause, no space for reflection. Leaders move from one fire to another, mistaking speed for effectiveness.

Urgency temporarily compensates for insufficient structure. It creates movement, but not stability. Over time, urgency exhausts people, erodes judgment, and prevents long-term thinking.

Urgency is not evidence of importance. It is often evidence of insufficient capacity.

Leaders Becoming Bottlenecks

Another sign of capacity failure is when leaders become the point through which everything must pass.

Decisions stall unless the leader approves them. Problems remain unresolved unless the leader intervenes. Progress slows when the leader is absent.

At first, this is mistaken for dedication or competence. In reality, it signals that responsibility has outgrown the system designed to carry it.

When leaders become bottlenecks, it is not because they are indispensable. It is because capacity has not been distributed.

Leadership was never meant to absorb everything. It was meant to govern distribution.

Emotional Volatility at Scale

As responsibility increases, emotional demands intensify. Leaders without sufficient emotional capacity often display volatility, irritability, defensiveness, withdrawal, or disproportionate reactions.

This is not a character flaw. It is overload.

Emotional volatility emerges when pressure exceeds the leader's ability to process it. The issue is not emotion itself, but the absence of internal structure to metabolize emotional weight without distortion.

At scale, unmanaged emotional load leaks into culture, communication, and decision-making.

Systems That Require Heroics to Function

When systems only work because someone is sacrificing constantly, capacity has already been exceeded.

Heroics are often celebrated in the short term. Over time, they become unsustainable.

Systems that rely on exceptional effort rather than sound design collapse when the hero becomes tired, distracted, or unavailable.

If success depends on exhaustion, the system is fragile. Capacity allows systems to function without constant rescue.

Success That Cannot Be Repeated

One of the most revealing signs of insufficient capacity is success that cannot be replicated.

A strong quarter followed by instability. A breakthrough year followed by decline. A successful initiative that cannot be sustained.

This indicates that success occurred through effort, favor, or circumstance, not through structure.

Capacity turns success into pattern. Without capacity, success remains episodic.

Capacity Failure Is Often Misdiagnosed

What makes capacity failure dangerous is that it is rarely identified correctly.

Burnout is labeled a motivation problem. Instability is called incompetence. Overwhelm is spiritualized or moralized. Collapse is treated as sudden rather than cumulative.

In truth, most failures are not moral, emotional, or intellectual. They are architectural.

When sustained pressure exceeds structure, failure is not surprising, it is inevitable.

Capacity Exists in Levels, Not Absolutes

Capacity is not a fixed trait. It is contextual.

A person may have sufficient capacity at one level of responsibility and insufficient capacity at another. This does not mean they are incapable—it means the demands have changed.

Capacity must always be evaluated relative to responsibility.

Capacity at the Level of the Individual Contributor

At the individual contributor level, capacity is primarily task-oriented. It involves managing personal workload, meeting expectations, maintaining consistency, and sustaining performance under supervision. Success here depends largely on discipline, competence, and reliability.

Many people perform well at this level because responsibility remains contained.

Capacity at the Level of the Team Leader

At the team level, capacity shifts.

Responsibility expands beyond personal output to include: managing personalities, resolving conflict, coordinating effort, absorbing dissatisfaction, maintaining morale while enforcing standards.

Personal success does not automatically translate into the ability to manage people. This is a different capacity altogether.

Many stall here—not because they cannot lead, but because they were never required to develop emotional, relational, and interpretive capacity before.

Capacity at the Organizational Level

At the organizational level, leadership becomes systemic.

Responsibility includes: designing structures, governing processes, managing interdependencies, sustaining culture, making decisions with incomplete information.

Here, leaders are accountable not only for outcomes, but for how outcomes are produced.

Skill matters less than coherence. Effort matters less than architecture.

Capacity Is Level-Specific, Not Identity-Defining

A critical truth must be stated clearly: Lacking capacity at a higher level does not negate value at a current one.

Many people misinterpret capacity limits as personal failure. In reality, capacity simply reveals where structure must be strengthened before expansion occurs.

Growth is not invalidated by delay. Delay is often evidence of wisdom.

Why This Distinction Matters

When leaders fail to recognize capacity mismatches, they respond incorrectly:

They push harder instead of redesigning, they blame people instead of systems, and they spiritualize strain instead of addressing structure.

Understanding how capacity shows up, and fails, allows leaders to intervene before collapse, not after.

This is the difference between managing outcomes and governing sustainability.

The Container Principle

Capacity functions like a container.

Whatever is poured into a container: authority, resources, opportunity or, responsibility, will only be held to the limit of that container's size and strength. When capacity is insufficient, increase becomes spillage rather than abundance.

This is why growth without capacity feels chaotic. It is not that increase is wrong. It is that the container was never designed to hold it.

The question is not whether opportunity exists. The question is whether vessels exist.

Capacity Versus Performance

Performance is episodic. Capacity is continuous.

Performance answers: Can this be done? Capacity answers: Can this be carried repeatedly without damage?

Many people perform well under urgency. Crisis creates adrenaline. Deadlines sharpen focus. Novelty sustains engagement. But urgency masks capacity gaps only temporarily. Over time, urgency exhausts what structure should sustain.

Capacity replaces urgency with stability.

Capacity Is Progressive, Not Overnight

One of the most damaging misconceptions about capacity is the belief that it is an overnight achievement. Capacity is not activated by promotion, opportunity, or insight. It is developed progressively—line upon line, layer upon layer—provided the mindset honors growth rather than impatience.

Capacity unfolds through measured exposure.

A powerful illustration of this principle is movement through increasing depth. At first, the environment is shallow—manageable, familiar, safe. With continued movement, depth increases gradually. Eventually, a point is reached where what could once be navigated easily now requires full engagement.

Depth is not reached by force. It is reached by progression.

No one begins fully immersed. Capacity grows through exposure that stretches without overwhelming—when the mindset allows the process to do its work.

Measurement: The Difference between Growth and Strain

What makes progressive depth instructive is measurement.

Movement is not reckless. Distance is observed. Depth is assessed. Adjustment occurs before collapse. This reveals a critical leadership principle:

Capacity expands when growth is measured, not rushed.

Unmeasured growth produces strain. Measured growth allows adaptation.

Many leaders move too far, too fast, without measuring what they are carrying or becoming. Speed is mistaken for progress. Visibility is confused with depth. The result is arrival at places where functioning is possible but sustainability is not.

Capacity-building requires pacing. It requires knowing when to advance, when to pause, and when to reinforce existing structure before proceeding.

Capacity and Mindset

Progress alone does not guarantee capacity. The mindset with which progress is approached determines whether growth stabilizes or destabilizes.

A mindset that demands instant mastery resists developmental stages. A mindset that honors progression adapts at each level.

Capacity grows when leaders understand:

i.   Early stages feel underwhelming,

ii. Middle stages feel stretching,

iii. Later stages feel demanding,

iv. Full immersion feels weighty.

Skipping stages does not accelerate maturity. It undermines it.

A Lived Illustration: Capacity Built on the Mountain

I vividly remember the first time I attempted to hike Kennesaw Mountain.

I was unprepared for the demand. Within minutes, my breathing was labored. My legs burned. My body protested every step forward. Turning back felt like a rational option. I genuinely thought I might not make it to the top.

I did not stop because it was easy. I continued because stopping would have cost me something internally.

Eventually, I reached the summit. The view was breathtaking. It became both my reward and my incentive. I had survived, not because I was strong, but because I endured.

The second climb was not easy either. But it was different. My body remembered what my mind had not yet processed. Over time, something subtle occurred. Without a dramatic moment or conscious declaration, climbing the mountain became manageable.

Eventually, it became routine. Then habitual. Then almost effortless.

What once felt life-threatening became second nature.

I did not develop capacity overnight. I developed it over time.

This is how capacity works.

The mountain did not change. My structure did.

Capacity as a Function of Weight, Time, and Repetition

Capacity cannot be understood apart from weight, time, and repetition. Any definition of capacity that ignores these three elements will remain incomplete and misleading.

Most people assess capacity based on isolated moments: a successful project, a breakthrough season, a visible achievement. **But capacity is not revealed in moments. It is revealed in duration.**

A structure that holds weight for one hour is not the same as a structure that holds weight for ten years. A leader who performs under pressure once is not the same as a leader who remains stable under pressure repeatedly. Capacity is not proven by surviving an event; it is proven by sustaining responsibility without deterioration.

This is why capacity must be understood as longitudinal, not episodic.

Capacity and Weight

Every level of responsibility introduces weight. Weight is not only workload. It includes:

i.   Decision consequence

ii. Moral responsibility

iii. Emotional exposure

iv. Relational tension

v.   Reputational risk

vi. Systemic dependency.

As responsibility increases, weight becomes less visible but more consequential. At lower levels, mistakes are localized. At higher levels, mistakes ripple.

Capacity determines whether weight is distributed or concentrated.

When capacity is insufficient, weight collapses inward. The leader becomes the shock absorber for everything:

i.   Every failure,

ii. Every conflict,

iii. Every unresolved issue,

iv. Every emotional burden.

This is why leaders without sufficient capacity often become controlling, exhausted, or isolated. They are not flawed; they are overloaded.

Capacity does not remove weight. It redistributes it.

Capacity and Time

Time is the most honest examiner of capacity.

Many people appear capable in short bursts. Urgency creates adrenaline. Crisis activates focus. Novelty sustains engagement. But time strips away adrenaline and exposes structure.

Capacity answers questions that only time can ask: Can this leader remain consistent? Can this system function without constant intervention? Can this organization survive success? Can this responsibility be carried without moral erosion?

Time reveals whether what looks like strength is actually stamina.

This is why capacity-building cannot be rushed. Growth that outpaces time creates fragility. Structures must be allowed to experience pressure long enough to reveal weaknesses before expansion continues.

Capacity and Repetition

Capacity is also revealed through repetition.

Doing something once is not the same as doing it repeatedly. Repetition introduces fatigue, variation, and unpredictability. It exposes whether systems are resilient or merely reactive.

In leadership, repetition looks like:

   i.   Managing conflict again and again

   ii. Making unpopular decisions repeatedly

   iii. Carrying other people's failures consistently

   iv. Showing up when outcomes are uncertain.

Repetition without collapse is a sign of capacity.

This is why some leaders succeed early but decline later. Early success often lacks repetition. Over time, unresolved gaps compound.

Capacity absorbs repetition without resentment.

Capacity Is the Ability to Remain Functional When Conditions Are No Longer Favorable

Another way to understand capacity is this:

Capacity is the ability to remain functional when conditions are no longer favorable. When support decreases. When praise disappears. When resources tighten. When outcomes are delayed. When pressure becomes routine.

Many leaders function well in favorable conditions. Capacity is revealed when those conditions are removed.

This distinction matters deeply in governance, healthcare, and systems leadership, where conditions are rarely ideal and often deteriorate before improving.

Capacity and Complexity

As leadership responsibility increases, complexity multiplies.

Complexity is not complication. Complication can be solved with expertise. Complexity cannot. It must be managed, not eliminated.

Complexity includes:

i.   Competing priorities,

ii. Conflicting interests,

iii. Incomplete information,

iv. Moral ambiguity, v. systemic interdependence.

Capacity allows leaders to function without demanding clarity prematurely. Leaders with low capacity oversimplify. Leaders with higher capacity tolerate tension while seeking coherence.

This is why intelligence alone is insufficient. Intelligence solves problems. Capacity carries unresolved complexity without panic.

Capacity and Emotional Load

Every leadership role carries an emotional load.

This load includes:

i. Disappointment from others,

ii. Dissatisfaction you cannot resolve,

iii. Criticism you must absorb,

iv. Loneliness of decision-making, v. restraint in expression.

Capacity determines whether emotional load is processed or internalized.

Leaders with insufficient capacity either discharge emotional weight onto others or suppress it until it erupts. Leaders with developed capacity metabolize emotional load without distortion.

This is not personality; it is structure.

Capacity Is Not the Absence of Strain

One of the most dangerous misunderstandings about capacity is the belief that it eliminates strain. It does not.

Capacity does not remove pressure. It prevents pressure from causing damage.

Strain is inevitable at higher levels. Capacity determines whether strain becomes strengthening or destructive.

A muscle grows by resistance. A structure fails by overload. Capacity-building is learning the difference.

Capacity and the Myth of Effort

Effort is often mistaken for capacity.

Effort can compensate temporarily for structural weakness. It cannot replace structure long-term. Effort relies on personal energy. Capacity relies on design.

This is why leaders who rely heavily on effort often burn out. They are personally sustaining what should be structurally supported.

Effort asks, "How much more can I give?" Capacity asks, "What needs to change so this is no longer dependent on me?"

Capacity as Predictive Architecture

Capacity allows leaders to predict outcomes before they occur.

If you understand:

i. How much weight a system can carry, i

ii. How much pressure a leader can absorb,

iii. How much complexity an organization can manage, then outcomes are no longer surprising.

Failure is rarely mysterious. It is structural.

Capacity explains not just what happens, but why it happens when it does.

Why Capacity Must Be Defined Before It Is Built

Without a precise definition, people attempt to build capacity by:

i. Increasing activity

ii. Expanding visibility

iii. Acquiring credentials

iv. Working longer hours.

These may increase exposure, but they do not increase sustainability.

Capacity-building requires:

i. Restraint before expansion

ii. Reinforcement before scaling

iii. Governance before growth

iv. Mindset before movement.

Transition toward Mindset

Once capacity is understood as weight-bearing architecture over time, the next realization becomes unavoidable:

Capacity does not collapse first at the level of skill, intelligence, or opportunity. It collapses first at the level of interpretation. Two people can face the same responsibility, the same pressure, the same opportunity—and respond entirely differently. One adapts. The other resists. One expands. The other contracts. The difference is not external. It is internal.

If Chapter 2 explains what capacity is and how it behaves, the next question becomes unavoidable:

Why do some people build capacity while others sabotage it, even with access, talent, and opportunity?

The answer lies in the mind.

The mind decides what feels possible, what feels threatening, what feels valuable, and what feels unnecessary. It determines whether opportunity is experienced as invitation or intrusion.

CHAPTER 3

◆————————————◆

Mindset: The Gatekeeper of Capacity

——

O pportunities do not stall because of scarcity—they stall because of mindset.

Capacity does not fail first at the level of skill, intelligence, or opportunity. It fails first at the level of interpretation. Two people can encounter the same responsibility, the same pressure, the same opportunity, and experience entirely different outcomes. One adapts. The other resists. One expands. The other contracts. The difference is not external. It is internal.

Capacity is architecture, but mindset is the blueprint that determines how that architecture is designed, reinforced, or undermined. Structures rarely collapse because they are weak; they collapse because they were built on assumptions that could not sustain weight. In the same way, leaders, systems, and institutions often fail not because opportunity was too large, but because mindset was too narrow to interpret growth accurately.

If capacity determines what can be carried, mindset determines how responsibility is perceived. And perception governs behavior long before outcomes become visible.

The Mind as the Gatekeeper of Growth

Every opportunity passes through the mind before it becomes reality.

Before responsibility is accepted, the mind interprets it. Before collaboration occurs, the mind evaluates trust. Before growth is sustained, the mind assigns meaning to pressure.

The mind decides what feels possible, what feels threatening, what feels valuable, and what feels unnecessary. It determines whether opportunity is experienced as invitation or intrusion.

This is why capacity-building cannot succeed without mindset transformation. Structures can be designed, systems can be introduced, and resources can be added, but if the mind resists expansion, growth will stall or fracture.

Mindset is not an accessory to leadership. It is the operating system beneath it.

Conscious and Subconscious Mind: Where Capacity Is Quietly Shaped

One of the most misunderstood aspects of mindset is the distinction between the conscious and subconscious mind.

The conscious mind is intentional. It is where goals are articulated, plans are formed, and commitments are made. It is logical, aspirational, and future-oriented.

The subconscious mind is interpretive. It stores memory, emotion, meaning, and learned responses. It is where experience becomes expectation and repetition becomes belief.

Most people attempt to build capacity consciously: through effort, discipline, and intention. Meanwhile their subconscious mind quietly resists change based on past experiences, fear, trauma, or misinterpretation.

This is why people say: "I want to grow," yet avoid responsibility. "I want leadership," yet resist accountability. "I want collaboration," yet struggle to trust. "I want expansion," yet fear visibility.

The conflict is not hypocrisy. It is misalignment.

Capacity expands when the conscious desire for growth aligns with a subconscious belief that growth is safe, possible, and sustainable.

Conditioning: When the Past Teaches the Mind to Stay Small

One of the most powerful forces shaping mindset is conditioning. Conditioning occurs when repeated experiences teach the mind what to expect, and more importantly, what not to attempt.

This conditioning does not require overt trauma. It forms through repetition:

i. Repeated failure

ii. Repeated rejection

iii. Repeated punishment for risk

iv. Repeated betrayal of trust

v. Repeated disappointment after effort.

Over time, the mind learns restraint not as wisdom, but as survival.

People stop testing boundaries not because they lack strength, but because experience has taught them that effort does not pay. Capacity remains, but belief contracts.

This is how individuals, leaders, and even institutions live far beneath their potential, not because they lack resources, but because their mindset has been trained to stay within familiar limits.

The Elephant and the Plastic Chair: Learned Limitation

There is a story of a young elephant tied with a rope to a small plastic chair. As a calf, the elephant struggles to pull free, but the rope holds. After repeated failed attempts, the elephant stops trying. Over time, the elephant grows, larger, stronger, vastly more powerful, yet the rope remains the same.

As an adult, capable of uprooting trees, the elephant remains tethered. Not by the rope, but by belief.

At some point, the limitation ceased to be physical and became psychological.

This illustrates one of the most dangerous forms of mindset captivity: learned limitation. At some point in the past, effort failed. Resistance proved painful. The mind concluded, this is as far as I go.

Capacity did not disappear. It was simply never tested again.

Many leaders operate like this elephant. They carry strength they no longer attempt to use. They live within boundaries that no longer apply. Their capacity has grown, but their mindset has not.

When Conditioning Becomes Identity

The most destructive effect of conditioning is that it eventually becomes identity.

People stop saying: "I failed before," and start saying: "This is not for me." They stop saying: "That environment limited me," and start saying: "I'm just not that kind of person."

Once limitation becomes identity, growth feels like betrayal rather than development. Capacity-building now threatens self-concept, not just comfort.

This is why mindset work must disentangle identity from past outcomes. Who you were forced to be in one season is not who you are designed to be forever.

The Eagle Raised Among Chickens: Exposure Precedes Expansion

Another illustration of mindset limitation is the story of an eagle raised among chickens. From birth, the eagle grows in an environment where pecking the ground is normal. It observes chickens scratching for food, flapping weak wings, and never leaving the earth. The eagle does the same.

Not because it lacks wings. Not because it lacks strength. But because it imitates what it sees.

The eagle has capacity to soar but no reference point for flight.

One day, the eagle sees another eagle soaring overhead. Recognition precedes action. Awareness precedes movement. The eagle attempts to imitate what it sees, and discovers what it was always capable of.

This reveals a critical leadership truth: exposure activates capacity.

Many people do not fail because they lack ability. They fail because they lack models that expand belief.

Environment as a Shaper of Mindset

Mindset is not formed in isolation. It is shaped by environment.

Environments teach:

i. What is normal

ii. What is rewarded

iii. What is punished

iv. What is possible

v. What is dangerous.

When environments normalize limitation, people internalize it as realism. When environments punish initiative, people equate restraint with maturity. When environments reward survival rather than growth, endurance is mistaken for capacity.

This is why growth often begins with environmental change: mentally, relationally, or structurally. New environments provide new reference points. They challenge inherited assumptions.

The eagle did not change its wings. It changed its awareness.

Problem-Focused Mindsets: When the Mind Blocks Opportunity

One of the most common capacity inhibitors is a problem-focused mindset.

This mindset does not lack intelligence. In fact, it often appears insightful. It identifies risks quickly. It anticipates obstacles. It detects flaws early.

But it does so at the expense of possibility.

Every opportunity is met with:

i.   "Here's why it won't work."

ii. "Here's what could go wrong."

iii. "Here's what we tried before."

iv. "Here's why this is risky."

Over time, the person becomes known as cautious or realistic. In reality, the mind has been trained to prioritize threat over growth.

This mindset does not eliminate problems. It magnifies them.

Capacity requires a mindset that can acknowledge risk without being governed by it.

Past Incarceration and the Mind's Memory

Past experiences of confinement, physical, social, or psychological, leave deep imprints on mindset.

Incarceration often conditions the mind toward:

i. Hyper-vigilance,

ii. Mistrust,

iii. Fear of exposure,

iv. Expectation of punishment,

v. Avoidance of visibility.

Even after release, the mind continues to operate as though freedom is conditional. Opportunity feels unsafe. Authority feels suspicious. Structure feels threatening.

Capacity exists, but mindset interprets expansion as danger.

This is not a character flaw. It is an unprocessed survival response.

Capacity-building here requires rehabilitation of belief, not motivation.

Subconscious Scripts: The Quiet Saboteurs

The subconscious mind runs on scripts, unspoken rules learned through experience.

Examples include:

i. "If I try and fail, I will be humiliated."

ii. "If I succeed, I will be targeted."

iii. "If I trust, I will be betrayed." I

iv. "If I stand out, I will lose safety."

These scripts operate silently, yet they determine behavior more powerfully than conscious intention.

This is why positive thinking fails. Capacity-building requires awareness, exposure, and reframing—not denial.

Mindset and Change: Why Capacity Resists Movement

One of the clearest indicators of mindset is how a person responds to change.

Change is not merely external adjustment. It is internal disruption. It challenges familiarity, exposes inadequacy, and demands reinterpretation of identity. For this reason, many people who desire growth subconsciously resist the very changes that make growth possible.

> *Capacity does not grow in static environments. It grows where change is engaged deliberately.*

Yet resistance to change is rarely framed as fear. It is often rationalized as:

i. Caution

ii. Wisdom

iii. Realism

iv. Patience

v. Principle.

In reality, resistance to change is often the mind attempting to preserve familiarity rather than pursue expansion.

This is why opportunities stall even when they are accessible. The mind is not prepared to reconfigure itself for a new level of responsibility.

Change Requires Cognitive Flexibility

Cognitive flexibility is the mind's ability to adapt interpretation when circumstances evolve. It allows a person to revise assumptions, update beliefs, and abandon methods that once worked but no longer apply.

Capacity-building requires cognitive flexibility because:

i. Every new level introduces unfamiliar demands

ii. Old strategies lose effectiveness,

iii. New tensions emerge that cannot be solved with prior tools.

Rigid minds treat change as a threat. Flexible minds treat change as information.

This distinction is critical. Leaders with rigid mindsets interpret change as instability. Leaders with flexible mindsets interpret it as instruction.

Capacity expands where learning replaces defensiveness.

Choices: The Repetitive Acts That Build or Erode Capacity

Capacity is not shaped primarily by major decisions. It is shaped by repeated small choices.

Every choice reinforces a mindset:

i. Choosing comfort over stretch

ii. Choosing control over collaboration

iii. Choosing speed over sustainability

iv. Choosing familiarity overgrowth.

These choices seem insignificant in isolation. Over time, they become patterns. Patterns become habits. Habits become structures. Structures become capacity—or limitation.

People often believe capacity-building requires dramatic action. In reality, it requires consistent alignment.

The mountain is not climbed in one leap. It is climbed step by step, often imperceptibly. Capacity grows the same way.

Decision-Making as a Capacity Indicator

Decision-making reveals capacity more accurately than performance.

When capacity is low, decisions are:

i. Reactive

ii. Emotionally driven

iii. Short-term focused

iv. Avoidance-oriented.

When capacity is growing, decisions become:

i. Deliberate

ii. Principle-based

iii. Long-term oriented

iv. System-aware.

Capacity is not measured by how quickly decisions are made, but by how well they account for weight, consequence, and sustainability.

This is why leadership maturity is evident not in decisiveness alone, but in discernment.

The Cost of Avoided Decisions

Avoidance is one of the most underestimated capacity killers.

When decisions are postponed, to avoid discomfort, pressure does not disappear, it accumulates. Deferred decisions compound complexity and transfer weight to the future.

Avoidance often masquerades as patience. In truth, it is often fear of consequence or loss of control.

Capacity grows when leaders develop the ability to make difficult decisions early, before urgency replaces wisdom.

Mindset and Responsibility Reinterpretation

Capacity expands when responsibility is reinterpreted correctly.

Many people associate responsibility with:

i.   Loss of freedom,

ii. Increased scrutiny

iii. Emotional burden

iv. Inevitable failure.

This interpretation produces resistance.

In reality, responsibility is stewardship. It is the authority to influence outcomes, shape systems, and create stability for others.

When the mind interprets responsibility as threat, capacity contracts. When it interprets responsibility as stewardship, capacity expands.

This is why two people can receive the same promotion: one flourishes, the other collapses.

Change, Choice, and the Fear of Visibility

Visibility introduces a unique form of pressure. It increases accountability, exposure, and consequence. For many, visibility triggers subconscious fear shaped by past experiences of judgment, punishment, or betrayal.

As a result, people unconsciously make choices that limit exposure:

i.   Declining opportunities

ii. Remaining behind the scenes

iii. Avoiding leadership roles

iv. Minimizing impact.

Capacity-building requires confronting fear of visibility. Growth cannot occur entirely in obscurity.

This does not mean reckless exposure. It means intentional engagement with responsibility despite discomfort.

Choice Architecture: Designing Decisions That Support Capacity

Capacity is not built by willpower alone. It is supported by choice architecture, the deliberate design of environments, routines, and structures that make aligned decisions easier.

People fail to build capacity not because they lack discipline, but because their environment reinforces misaligned choices.

Capacity-building requires:

i.   Environments that reward growth,

ii. Structures that support reflection,

iii. Systems that reduce unnecessary friction,

iv. Accountability that reinforces alignment.

Choice architecture transforms intention into consistency.

When Past Choices Become Present Constraints

Every present limitation was once a choice—either made or avoided.

This is not blame. It is agency.

Understanding this reframes capacity-building from fate to responsibility. Capacity can be rebuilt because it was built before—consciously or unconsciously.

Past choices may explain present constraints, but they do not justify permanent stagnation.

Mindset and the Willingness to Rechoose

One of the most powerful capacity-building moments is the willingness to rechoose.

To rechoose:

i.   Collaboration over isolation,

ii. Structure over chaos,

iii. Patience over urgency,

iv. Growth over familiarity.

Rechoosing requires humility. It acknowledges that what once felt protective may now be restrictive.

Capacity expands when leaders allow themselves to evolve beyond earlier versions of themselves.

Change Is the Environment Where Capacity Grows

Capacity does not grow in comfort. It grows in negotiated discomfort, where stretch is intentional and collapse is prevented.

This is why mindset must be addressed thoroughly before capacity-building strategies are introduced.

Without mindset transformation:

i.   Change feels threatening

ii. Choices feel costly

iii. Decisions feel risky.

With mindset alignment:

i.   Change becomes instructive,

ii. Choices become strategic

iii. Decisions become stabilizing.

Capacity-building is not a single event. It is a cumulative process shaped by mindset, change engagement, repeated choices, and disciplined decision-making.

The mind is the first structure that must be reinforced.

Without this work, capacity remains theoretical. With it, capacity becomes inevitable.

In the next chapter, we will move from mindset into behavioral patterns and leadership habits, examining how internal alignment produces external consistency.

Because capacity is not built by intention alone. It is built by aligned thinking, repeated choice, and disciplined response to change.

Mindset and Value Perception: Why the Woman Did Not See the Oil

The woman with the oil did not lack provision. She lacked valuation.

She normalized what should have been leveraged. She minimized what should have been multiplied. Familiarity dulled perception.

Many leaders undervalue what they carry because it has always been present. Capacity often begins not with acquisition, but with revaluation.

Mindset determines what is seen as ordinary versus strategic.

Growth Requires Mindset Expansion before Structural Expansion

Without mindset expansion:

i. Delegation feels like loss,

ii. Collaboration feels unsafe

iii. Accountability feels threatening

iv. Growth feels destabilizing.

This is why due diligence at the mindset level is non-negotiable. Structures built without mindset alignment eventually collapse.

The Threshold Question

Before moving forward, a critical question must be asked:

Where has my mind stopped testing my strength? Where have past experiences taught restraint that no longer applies? Where have survival strategies become permanent identities?

Capacity exists. Opportunity exists.

The question is whether the mind is willing to expand.

Transition Forward

In the next chapter, we move from internal architecture to external expression, examining how mindset translates into habits, leadership behavior, and systemic outcomes.

Because capacity does not fail all at once. It fails first in thought, then in behavior, then in structure, then in outcomes.

And when mindset is addressed thoroughly, capacity can finally grow without sabotage.

Capacity–Mindset Diagnostic Scale (CMDS)

Purpose

This tool measures mindset readiness for capacity expansion. It does not measure talent, intelligence, or motivation. It evaluates whether the mental architecture required to carry greater responsibility is in place.

Use this tool before attempting to scale leadership, systems, or opportunity.

How to Use This Scale

For each statement, rate yourself on a scale of 1 to 5 based on patterned behavior, not intention.

1. Strongly Disagree

2. Disagree

3. Neutral / Inconsistent

4. Agree

5. Strongly Agree

Be honest. Capacity is limited by self-deception more than by weakness.

Domain 1: Change Orientation (Mindset response to disruption and transition)

1. I can engage change without immediately interpreting it as instability.

2. I adapt my thinking when circumstances shift, even if past methods worked.

3. I can release familiar structures without emotional distress.

4. I see change as information, not interruption.

5. I can grow without needing everything to feel settled first.

Domain Insight Low scores here indicate rigidity, not lack of intelligence. Capacity cannot expand where the mind resists movement.

Domain 2: Choice Discipline (How repeated decisions shape capacity)

1. I consistently choose long-term sustainability over short-term relief.

2. I do not rely on urgency to stay productive.

3. I make difficult choices early rather than postponing discomfort.

4. My daily decisions align with the future I want to sustain.

5. I recognize when comfort is limiting growth.

Domain Insight Capacity is built by repeated small choices, not dramatic moments.

Domain 3: Decision-Making Under Weight (Ability to govern responsibility without reactivity)

1. I can make decisions without needing emotional validation.

2. I tolerate ambiguity without rushing premature clarity.

3. I can disappoint others without internal collapse.

4. I separate personal worth from outcome results.

5. I remain functional when decisions carry consequence.

Domain Insight Low scores signal capacity strain, not incompetence. Decision-making reveals capacity more than performance.

Domain 4: Responsibility Interpretation (Burden vs stewardship mindset)

1. I interpret responsibility as stewardship, not punishment.

2. I can carry accountability for outcomes I did not personally create.

3. Increased responsibility does not make me feel trapped.

4. I do not personalize systemic failures.

5. I am comfortable being answerable at scale.

Domain Insight Capacity collapses when responsibility is interpreted as threat.

Domain 5: Trust, Collaboration, and Delegation (Relational capacity for scale)

1. I trust others to carry responsibility without micromanagement.

2. I can collaborate without fear of loss of control.

3. Past betrayals do not dictate present leadership behavior.

4. Systems I lead function in my absence.

5. Delegation expands my effectiveness rather than threatening my relevance.

Domain Insight Low scores indicate isolation-based leadership, a major capacity ceiling.

Domain 6: Past Conditioning Awareness (Subconscious scripts and learned limitation)

I am aware of how past experiences shape my current decisions. I do not confuse survival strategies with identity. I actively challenge internal narratives that limit growth. I can distinguish caution from fear. My past does not define the size of my future.

Domain Insight Unexamined conditioning silently governs capacity.

Domain 7: Value Perception (Ability to recognize and leverage what already exists)

1. I accurately recognize the value of what I already carry.

2. Familiarity does not cause me to undervalue resources.

3. I can identify latent assets in people and systems.

4. I believe expansion often begins with reconfiguration, not acquisition.

5. I revisit assumptions about what is "ordinary."

Domain Insight Capacity often begins with revaluation, not new provision.

Domain 8: Emotional Regulation at Scale (Stability under pressure and visibility)

1. I process emotional load without suppressing or discharging it onto others.

2. Increased visibility does not destabilize me.

3. Criticism does not impair my clarity.

4. I do not rely on praise to remain functional.

5. Pressure strengthens rather than fragments my leadership.

Domain Insight Capacity metabolizes emotional weight without distortion.

Domain 9: Sustainability Architecture (Time, repetition, endurance)

1. My current pace is sustainable over years, not months.

2. My effectiveness does not depend on constant personal effort.

3. Rest and reflection are structurally built into my life.

4. Success in my life is repeatable, not accidental.

5. Growth has not eroded my integrity or health.

Domain Insight Sustainability is the truest test of capacity.

Scoring Interpretation

Total Possible Score: 225

180–225: High-Capacity Readiness You possess the mindset architecture required for expanded responsibility. Growth can be scaled with structure and systems.

140–179: Transitional Capacity You can grow, but certain mindset domains will limit sustainability. Expansion without reinforcement will create strain.

100–139: Restricted Capacity Opportunity may arrive, but sustainability is at risk. Mindset rehabilitation must precede growth.

Below 100: Capacity Vulnerability Growth at this stage will likely lead to overwhelm or collapse. Focus on mindset alignment before pursuing expansion.

> *Capacity is not limited by opportunity. It is limited by the mind's readiness to govern what arrives.*

Until a belief is embodied through consistent behavior, it has not become capacity. It remains intention, well-meaning, intelligent, and ineffective.

CHAPTER 4

◆————————————◆

From Mindset to Habit

——

C apacity becomes real only when it becomes repeatable.

Capacity does not announce itself. It does not arrive with a title, a promotion, or a sudden sense of readiness. Capacity becomes visible only when what a person believes begins to shape what they do repeatedly—especially when conditions are inconvenient, pressure is sustained, and motivation is absent.

This is where many leadership conversations fail.

They stop at insight.

They assume that awareness equals transformation. They mistake understanding for readiness. They confuse inspiration with structure.

But capacity does not live in insight. It lives in habit.

Dr. Joke Solanke

Until a belief is embodied through consistent behavior, it has not become capacity. It remains intention, well-meaning, intelligent, and ineffective.

This chapter addresses the most neglected transition in leadership development: the movement from mindset to habit, from internal alignment to functional strength.

Habit as Embodied Belief

Every habit is a belief that has found a body.

People often think of habits as behavioral routines, things you do or stop doing. In reality, habits are the physical expression of what you believe to be true, necessary, or inevitable.

You do not repeatedly do what you agree with. You repeatedly do what you believe.

This distinction matters because capacity is not formed by agreement. It is formed by embodiment.

A leader may intellectually agree that rest is necessary—but if their habits communicate that exhaustion is normal, their true belief has already been declared.

A professional may affirm the value of delegation, but if they consistently override systems and re-insert themselves, their habits reveal a deeper belief: "Things only work if I do them myself."

Habit exposes belief without requiring language.

This is why capacity cannot be assessed solely by what leaders say they value. It must be assessed by what their habits support.

Why Insight without Habit Changes Nothing

One of the most persistent myths in leadership development is that insight leads to change.

Insight does not lead to change. Integration does.

People can:

i.   Attend trainings

ii. Read books

iii. Listen to teachings,

iv. Agree with frameworks and still remain structurally unchanged.

This is not resistance. It is reality.

Insight informs the mind. Habit trains the system.

Until insight is translated into repeatable behavior, it does not alter capacity. It merely increases cognitive awareness, sometimes increasing frustration rather than growth.

This is why many highly intelligent, well-informed leaders remain overwhelmed. They know what should change, but their habits keep reproducing the same outcomes.

Capacity is not built by knowing better. It is built by living differently, consistently.

Repetition as Neurological Alignment

Capacity is not only psychological. It is neurological.

The human brain is designed to strengthen what is repeated. Neural pathways become more efficient not through intensity, but through frequency.

This is why:

i. Sporadic excellence does not build capacity,

ii. Emotional breakthroughs do not sustain change,

iii. Moments of clarity fade without structure.

Repetition is how the brain learns what to prioritize.

When a leader consistently pauses before reacting, they are not just practicing restraint, they are rewiring response patterns.

When someone repeatedly structures their day rather than improvising under pressure, they are not just being organized, they are training their nervous system to function without urgency.

Capacity grows when repetition replaces reactivity.

This neurological reality explains why habit, not motivation, is the backbone of sustainable leadership.

Discipline vs Motivation: The Capacity Distinction

Motivation is emotional. Discipline is structural.

Motivation fluctuates with mood, energy, affirmation, and environment. Discipline functions regardless of these variables.

Leaders who rely on motivation to sustain growth eventually stall, not because they lack desire, but because desire cannot carry weight over time.

Discipline, by contrast, is the architecture that allows capacity to grow quietly and reliably.

This distinction appears repeatedly in leadership literature, including in The '7 Habits of Highly Effective People.' Stephen Covey did not frame effectiveness as a personality trait or an emotional state. He framed it as alignment between values and daily practices.

What Covey described as "private victory" before "public victory" is, at its core, a capacity principle: internal discipline precedes external effectiveness.

Discipline is not rigidity. It is repeatability.

Capacity is not built by doing more. It is built by doing the right things consistently, especially when no one is watching.

Why Leaders Resist Habit Formation

If habits are so powerful, why do capable people resist them?

Because habits remove illusion.

Habit exposes whether change is truly desired or merely admired.

Many leaders resist habit formation because:

i.   Habits reduce flexibility,

ii. Habits reveal priorities,

iii. Habits confront identity.

Improvisation allows people to preserve self-image. Structure demands honesty.

When habits are absent, leaders can attribute inconsistency to circumstances. When habits are present, outcomes become traceable.

Capacity grows where leaders are willing to be traceable.

Rhythm: The Overlooked Architecture of Capacity

One of the most practical yet neglected elements of capacity is rhythm.

Rhythm is the patterned distribution of effort, rest, focus, and recovery.

Leaders without rhythm rely on urgency to function. Leaders with rhythm rely on structure.

Rhythm determines:

i. How energy is conserved,

ii. How decisions are spaced,

iii. How pressure is absorbed

iv. How recovery occurs.

Without rhythm, even strong leaders burn out—not because they lack stamina, but because they lack pacing.

Capacity is not about always enduring maximum pressure. It is about sustaining functional performance over time.

Rhythm makes endurance possible.

Consistency over Intensity

Another capacity misconception is the belief that intensity accelerates growth.

Intensity produces spikes. Consistency produces stability.

Many leaders overestimate what intensity can do and underestimate what consistency can build.

A leader who occasionally performs at a high level does not have the same capacity as one who performs steadily over time.

Consistency is what converts potential into reliability.

This is why capacity is often invisible in its early stages. It does not announce itself dramatically. It accumulates quietly.

Capacity is built when leaders choose:

i.   Steady over spectacular

ii. Repeatable over impressive

iii. Sustainable over heroic.

Restraint: The Discipline Most Leaders Avoid

Restraint is one of the clearest indicators of capacity.

Leaders with low capacity often say yes too quickly. They overextend. They accept responsibilities they cannot sustain. They confuse opportunity with obligation.

Leaders with developed capacity practice restraint.

Restraint looks like:

i.   Declining opportunities that exceed current structure

ii. Postponing expansion until systems are ready

iii. Limiting visibility to preserve focus,

iv. Saying no to protect sustainability.

This is not fear. It is governance.

Restraint is the habit that prevents capacity collapse.

When Capacity Becomes Habitual: Comfort, Speed, and Mastery over Time

One of the clearest ways to understand how capacity becomes visible is through the transformation of discomfort into familiarity.

I became comfortable, and eventually fast, at climbing Kennesaw Mountain, a task that initially felt punishing, overwhelming, and physically impossible, not because the mountain changed, but because I changed.

At the beginning, every step demanded conscious effort. My breathing was labored. My legs protested. My pace was slow. I had to stop frequently, recalibrate, and question whether continuing was wise. The terrain felt hostile. The incline felt unforgiving. The distance felt deceptive.

At that stage, climbing was not a habit. It was an event.

But something subtle happened as I returned, again and again.

Without a formal declaration or a dramatic breakthrough, repetition began to do its quiet work. My body learned the rhythm of the incline. My lungs adapted to the demand. My muscles strengthened without my permission. What once required intense focus began to require less conscious negotiation.

Eventually, I noticed something startling.

I was no longer negotiating with the mountain. I was moving through it.

My pace increased, not because I was trying harder, but because my system had adapted. The pauses shortened. The discomfort no longer dominated my attention. What once felt like a threat began to feel familiar. What was once exhausting became manageable. Then routine. Then natural.

The task did not become easier. I became more capable.

This is how capacity works.

Capacity does not eliminate demand. It reduces friction.

Capacity does not remove strain. It changes how strain is processed.

And the mechanism that makes this transformation possible is habit.

Why Habit Changes the Experience of Weight

Habit changes how weight is experienced.

In the early stages of capacity-building, weight feels personal. Every demand feels like an assault on energy, competence, and confidence. But as habit forms, the same weight is redistributed across strengthened systems, physical, mental, emotional, and structural.

What once felt heavy no longer feels dramatic.

This is why seasoned leaders often appear calm under pressure. Not because pressure is absent, but because their systems are accustomed to carrying it.

Habit trains the body, the mind, and the nervous system to stop interpreting demand as danger.

Without habit, every challenge feels urgent. With habit, challenges become navigable.

From Event-Based Effort to Habitual Capacity

Many people approach growth as a series of events:

i. A training

ii. A retreat

iii. A breakthrough moment

iv. A promotion.

But capacity does not grow through events. It grows through patterns.

Events can inspire. Patterns transform.

This is why capacity remains elusive for people who rely on motivation rather than habit. Motivation fluctuates. Patterns endure.

Habit is what converts effort into infrastructure.

Steps to Building Habits That Create Capacity

Capacity-building habits do not form accidentally. They follow identifiable stages. Skipping these stages leads to frustration, inconsistency, and eventual abandonment.

Below is a practical, leadership-grade framework for habit formation that builds capacity rather than exhaustion.

1. Start with One Repeating Pressure Point

Capacity habits must be anchored to reality, not ideals.

Rather than asking, "What should I improve?", the more useful question is: "Where am I consistently strained?"

Strain reveals where capacity is insufficient.

Examples:

i.   Emotional strain during conflict

ii. Cognitive strain when decisions accumulate

iii. Physical strain from unsustainable schedules

iv. Relational strain from poor boundaries

v.   Structural strain from unclear roles.

The mountain did not become my habit all at once. It became my habit because it represented a repeatable point of resistance.

Capacity habits should be built where pressure already exists, not where it is imagined.

2. Reduce the Habit to a Repeatable Unit

One of the fastest ways to fail at habit formation is to make the habit too large.

Capacity does not grow through dramatic commitments. It grows through small, repeatable actions that compound.

In mountain climbing, the habit was not "conquer the mountain."

It was show up, take the first step, keep moving.

For leaders, this might look like:

i.   A daily pause before responding,

ii. A weekly review instead of constant reaction

iii. A scheduled boundary rather than ad hoc rest

iv. A consistent delegation practice rather than heroic rescue.

Capacity is built by actions small enough to repeat even on difficult days.

3. Attach the Habit to an Existing Rhythm

Habits that float independently are fragile.

Habits attached to existing rhythms endure.

This is why habit formation succeeds when it is integrated rather than added.

I did not create a separate identity for mountain climbing. It became part of my weekly rhythm. It was attached to time already reserved, energy already allocated, and intention already set.

In leadership, capacity habits attach best when they align with:

i.   Existing meetings

ii. Daily routines

iii. Weekly reviews

iv. Recurring pressure points.

Capacity grows when habits are embedded into life, not imposed on it.

4. Expect Discomfort without Interpreting It as Failure

One of the most important mindsets shift in habit-building is learning to expect discomfort without assigning meaning to it.

Early discomfort does not mean:

i.   The habit is wrong

ii. You are incapable

iii. Progress is failing.

It means adaptation is occurring.

When climbing first began, discomfort was information, not a verdict.

Capacity habits feel awkward before they feel natural. This is not resistance; it is neurological recalibration.

Those who quit early often misinterpret discomfort as disqualification.

5. Measure Consistency, Not Intensity

Capacity does not respond to intensity. It responds to consistency.

Climbing faster did not build capacity. Climbing regularly did.

This is why capacity-building habits must be evaluated by frequency, not effort.

Questions that matter: Did I return? Did I repeat? Did I maintain rhythm?

Over time, consistency changes baseline performance without conscious effort.

6. Allow Habit to Become Identity-Neutral

One of the quiet transformations of habit is that it removes drama from performance.

Eventually, I did not "prepare" to climb. I simply climbed.

This is when habit stops feeling like discipline and starts feeling like identity.

7. Increase Load Only After Stability Is Established

One of the most dangerous mistakes in capacity-building is increasing load too early.

Speed increased only after stability formed. Distance increased only after endurance adapted.

Capacity collapses when leaders add complexity before systems stabilize.

This applies to:

i.   Leadership scope

ii. Decision volume

iii. Emotional exposure

iv. Organizational scale.

Growth must follow stability, not precede it.

8. Recognize the Moment Habit Becomes Second Nature

There is a quiet moment in capacity-building when effort drops and fluency emerges.

No announcement marks it. No celebration interrupts it.

You simply realize that what once required negotiation now happens automatically.

That is capacity.

At that point, leaders often underestimate what has occurred. They assume nothing significant has changed because nothing dramatic happened.

But everything has changed.

The system has adapted.

Why Habit Is the Most Honest Measure of Capacity

People can perform occasionally without capacity. They cannot sustain capacity without habit.

Habit reveals:

i.   What has truly been integrated

ii. What the system can now carry

iii. What no longer requires force.

This is why habit is the most honest diagnostic of capacity.

Not intention. Not aspiration. Not belief.

Habit.

Capacity does not arrive suddenly. It arrives quietly, through repetition, restraint, and rhythm.

What once felt impossible becomes manageable. What once felt demanding becomes familiar. What once felt exhausting becomes routine.

The mountain remains the same.

But the one who climbs it is no longer who they were.

That is the power of habit.

And that is where capacity becomes visible.

Why Insight Feels Powerful but Fades

Insight produces emotional clarity. Habit produces functional change.

Insight feels powerful because it creates a sense of movement without cost. Habit requires cost.

Insight is instantaneous. Habit is incremental.

This explains why people often chase insight while avoiding habit. *Insight flatters the mind. Habit disciplines the self.*

But capacity does not respond to insight. It responds to repetition under constraint.

From Personal Insight to Organizational Habit

Capacity is not only personal. It scales.

Organizations develop capacity the same way individuals do, through habit.

An organization's capacity is revealed by:

i. How decisions are routinely made

ii. How conflict is consistently handled,

iii. How accountability is regularly enforced

iv. How rest and renewal are structurally protected.

Organizations that rely on heroic individuals rather than shared habits eventually fracture.

This is why strong individuals fail in weak systems.

Habit is how capacity becomes collective.

Why Leaders Become Bottlenecks without Habit

When leaders lack personal habit structures, they compensate by staying involved in everything.

They become the decision point, the problem solver, and the emotional regulator.

This is not leadership. It is load concentration.

Habit allows responsibility to be distributed. Without it, leaders absorb weight that should be shared.

Capacity increases when systems carry what individuals once carried alone.

Habit as the Bridge between Mindset and Structure

Mindset shapes belief. Habit translates belief into action. Structure preserves action over time.

Without habit, mindset remains theoretical. Without structure, habit remains fragile.

This chapter sits at the hinge point of the entire book because habit is where capacity becomes observable.

Not in vision statements. Not in aspirations. Not in intentions.

But in what is done again and again.

Why Capacity Becomes Trustworthy Only When It Is Repeatable

Trust, personal, organizational, or societal, is built on predictability.

People trust leaders whose responses are stable, whose systems are reliable, and whose habits are consistent.

Capacity becomes trustworthy only when it can be depended on under varying conditions.

Repeatability is the proof of capacity.

Capacity becomes real only when it becomes repeatable.

Until beliefs are embodied in habit, capacity remains potential, not structure.

From Goals to Systems: Why Habits Outperform Intentions

One of the most formative lessons in my own capacity development came from an unlikely place, an early online course at Kennesaw State University, taken long before virtual learning became common.

Before we were even allowed to enroll, we were required to complete a preparatory module. The purpose was not to test intelligence or motivation. It was to determine whether we could function within a system rather than rely on goals alone.

The instruction was simple but disruptive.

We were not asked to set academic goals. We were asked to build a study system.

Specifically, we were required to identify: the time of day when our concentration was highest, the duration we could sustain deep focus without mental fatigue, and the environmental conditions that supported clarity rather than distraction.

The goal was to study. The system was to make studying inevitable.

What became clear very quickly was this: two hours of focused, systematized study consistently produced better outcomes than ten hours of unfocused, reactive effort.

That experience fundamentally shifted how I understood capacity.

Capacity is not built by wanting to do something more. It is built by designing a system that makes the right behavior repeatable.

Out of that experience, I developed a habit that remains with me to this day. I began waking at, or before, 4:00 a.m. Between 4:00 and 7:00 a.m., the most cognitively demanding and strategically important tasks of my day were completed.

Even long after that course ended, the habit remained.

That system, more than motivation, more than goals, has made it possible for me to write, think, and lead effectively despite an otherwise demanding schedule.

This is the quiet power of systems.

Why Systems Thinking Is Essential for Capacity

Goals tell you what you want. Systems determine whether it happens consistently.

Most people fail at capacity-building because they rely on:

i.   Motivation instead of structure

ii. Intention instead of rhythm

iii. Effort instead of design.

Systems thinking shifts the question from: "What do I want to achieve?" to: "What structure will make this inevitable?"

Capacity does not respond to ambition. It responds to repeatable design.

What began as an academic requirement became a leadership principle.

The habit of protecting my highest-capacity hours did more for my growth than any motivational surge ever could. It taught me that systems outlive seasons, and habits formed under discipline continue to produce long after motivation fades.

This is why capacity-building must move beyond goals into systems.

Because what you can do once is performance. What your system supports daily is capacity.

Preparing for What Comes Next

Habit is where capacity becomes visible, but it is not where capacity becomes complete.

A leader may develop strong habits in one area and still collapse in another. Consistency in execution does not automatically translate to emotional regulation. Discipline in personal routines does not guarantee relational discernment. Operational efficiency does not ensure ethical resilience under pressure.

This is where many capable leaders become confused. They see progress, yet instability remains. They experience growth, yet strain persists. The issue is not that capacity has not been built, it is that it has been built unevenly.

Capacity is not singular. It is multidimensional.

Strength in one domain cannot compensate for weakness in another. Habits stabilize behavior, but capacity must exist across multiple dimensions if responsibility is to be carried without fracture.

In the next chapter, we move beyond habit formation into the five dimensions of capacity, personal, mental and emotional, relational, structural, and ethical. These dimensions reveal why leaders who "appear" disciplined can still fail, why systems with strong performers can still collapse, and why sustainable leadership requires more than consistency, it requires balance.

Because true capacity is not proven by how well one part of the system functions, but by how well the entire system holds together under pressure.

Tool: The Habit-to-Capacity System Builder

Purpose

This tool helps translate intention into habit and habit into capacity. It is not about doing more, it is about designing better.

Tool: The Habit-to-Capacity System Builder Purpose This tool helps translate intention into habit and habit into capacity. It is not about doing more—it is about designing better.

STEP 1: *Identify the Capacity Outcome (Not the Goal)*

Instead of asking "What do I want to do?" ask: What capacity must increase for my next level of responsibility?

Examples: Decision endurance Emotional regulation Strategic thinking Focused execution Writing or creative output Leadership presence

Write one capacity area:

_____

STEP 2: *Identify the High-Leverage Window*

Capacity grows fastest during periods of low distraction and high clarity.

Answer honestly:

_____

What time of day am I mentally sharpest?

_____

When is my energy most stable?

_____

When do interruptions decrease?

_____

My high-leverage window is: From _____ to

_____

STEP 3: Define the Smallest Repeatable Unit

Capacity grows through consistency, not intensity.

Ask: What is the smallest action I can repeat daily without resistance?

_____

What can I sustain even on difficult days?

_____

My daily habit unit: (Time-bound, specific, repeatable)

STEP 4: Design the Environment (Remove Friction)

Habits fail more often due to environment than willpower.

Ask: What distractions must be removed?

_____

What tools must be prepared in advance?

_____

What boundaries must be protected?

_____

Environmental adjustments:

STEP 5: *Attach the Habit to an Existing Rhythm*

Habits stick when they are anchored, not added.

This habit will occur:

☐ Before my day begins

☐ After an existing routine

☐ At the same time every day

☐ As the first task in my workday

Anchor point:

STEP 6: **Track Consistency, Not Performance**

Do not evaluate: quality output mood

Evaluate only: Did I show up?

Daily check (30 days):

☐ ☐

Capacity builds quietly.

STEP 7: *Review for Sustainability (Not Speed)*

After 30 days, ask: Does this feel less effortful?

Has resistance decreased?

Has clarity increased?

If yes → stabilize. If no → simplify, don't abandon.

Capacity is not formed by heroic effort. It is formed by intelligent repetition.

Capacity requirements are not universal; they are domain specific. What sustains effectiveness in one sphere may be completely insufficient in another.

—

CHAPTER 5

◆────────────────◆

Five Dimensions of Capacity Part I

──────

S trength in one dimension cannot compensate for collapse in another.

This chapter has been the most eye-opening for me personally. When I placed my own life and leadership against the capacity scorecard, what emerged was not failure, but clarity. I saw unmistakable room for improvement. I saw the need for balance, realignment, and recalibration—not because nothing was working, but because some areas were carrying more weight than they were designed to bear.

This chapter helps answer a question many leaders quietly wrestle with: Why does success in one area of life not automatically translate into success in another? The answer is capacity.

Capacity requirements are not universal; they are domain specific. What sustains effectiveness in one sphere may be completely insufficient in another.

Capacity cannot be built on deficiency. Deficiency must be addressed before capacity can be expanded. Attempting to build on weakness without first correcting it only creates instability. The principle is structural, not motivational.

It is like laying a foundation. A building constructed on a mountain, on a plain field, and along a seaside will each require different engineering considerations. The goal may be the same, but the demands of the terrain determine the design. Ignoring those differences does not change reality—it invites collapse.

In the same way, the same individual will require different capacity-building strategies depending on the domain in question. Personal stamina, emotional regulation, relational discernment, structural governance, and ethical resilience do not develop by accident, nor do they grow evenly.

This chapter introduces five dimensions of capacity that anchor every other area of leadership and life. While there may be additional areas of growth unique to individual contexts, these five dimensions provide a stable framework for assessment, correction, and intentional development. They explain why imbalance persists despite effort—and how alignment restores sustainability.

Capacity is not about doing more. It is about being built correctly for what you are carrying.

Dimension Two: Mental & Emotional Capacity (Regulation, Clarity, and Internal Stability)

If personal capacity asks whether a leader can carry weight, mental and emotional capacity asks a deeper question: Can the leader carry weight without being internally destabilized by it?

Many leaders possess stamina yet remain fragile. They stay busy, visible, and productive, but internally they are reactive, scattered, or emotionally exhausted. They function—but they do not govern themselves. Over time, responsibility does not sharpen them; it erodes them.

Mental and emotional capacity determines whether leadership pressure produces clarity or confusion, composure or volatility, wisdom or exhaustion.

This dimension answers a critical question: Can the leader remain internally stable while external pressure increases?

What Mental & Emotional Capacity Actually Is

Mental and emotional capacity is the leader's ability to regulate internal responses while navigating external demands. It includes the capacity to:

i.   Regulate emotional reactions under pressure

ii. Maintain cognitive clarity amid complexity

iii. Tolerate ambiguity without panic

iv. Process disappointment without distortion, and make decisions without being hijacked by fear, ego, or unresolved trauma.

It is not the absence of emotion. It is the governance of emotion.

It is not superior intelligence. It is clarity under load.

This capacity determines whether leadership refines judgment, or corrodes it.

Why Intelligence and Visibility Do Not Protect Leaders Here

High intelligence, public respect, and cultural influence are often mistaken for emotional stability. They are not the same.

Intelligence processes information. Emotional capacity governs interpretation.

This is why leaders with exceptional intellect or public impact can still unravel under sustained pressure. Emotional regulation does not automatically grow alongside influence. In fact, visibility often accelerates depletion by increasing exposure, scrutiny, and relational demand.

Public platforms apply continuous pressure: constant feedback, loss of narrative control, criticism without context, and relentless expectation. Leaders who lack emotional regulation experience this pressure as a threat to identity, not merely reputation.

When regulation collapses, reaction takes over.

This explains why some leaders "act a fool" on public platforms, becoming defensive, bullying critics, personalizing disagreement, or spiraling in full view. These behaviors are not signs of strength. They are signals of internal overload.

Why Some Leaders Take Everything Personal

Taking issues personally is a hallmark of low emotional differentiation.

Emotionally differentiated leaders can separate what is being said from who they are

Leaders without this capacity experience criticism as an attack on self, not feedback on function. Disagreement feels like disrespect. Accountability feels like betrayal. Correction feels like rejection.

This is why minor challenges escalate into public conflicts. The internal system cannot absorb the weight quietly.

Mental and emotional capacity provides leaders with options. Without it, leaders react from survival rather than strategy.

Why Others Can Remain Composed Under Abuse or Disrespect

At the opposite extreme are leaders who appear calm, even gracious under insult, misrepresentation, or hostility.

This is not passivity. It is emotional containment.

These leaders possess internal clarity, identity stability, and emotional boundaries. They are not numb; they are regulated. They do not need to dominate to feel safe. They do not need to retaliate to feel powerful.

Capacity gives leaders the freedom to choose restraint.

When Emotional Capacity Collapses Under Visibility

There is a sobering truth leaders must confront: public impact does not equal internal stability.

Some of the most gifted, respected, and influential individuals collapse not because they lacked purpose, success, or the ability to engage others, but because their mental and emotional capacity was exceeded over time without sufficient containment.

This pattern explains why leadership failure often appears confusing to observers.

How does someone so effective, so articulate, so admired unravel so publicly, or so privately?

The answer is not always moral failure. Often, it is capacity depletion.

The prophet Elijah's experience illustrates this clearly. After prolonged exposure to confrontation, responsibility, and isolation, he did not lose his calling, he lost emotional regulation. What followed was withdrawal, despair, distorted perception, and a desire to escape life itself. This was not rebellion. It was collapse under cumulative load.

This pattern is not ancient. It is current.

Many still wrestles with why Anthony Bourdain, a man with extraordinary cultural influence, intellectual depth, and the ability to connect meaningfully with millions, ended his own life. His public capacity was undeniable. His internal burden, less visible.

The ability to carry others does not automatically translate into the ability to carry oneself.

Sustained visibility, emotional exposure, relational intensity, travel, and the burden of meaning-making can quietly exhaust internal reserves, especially when a leader becomes the container for everyone else's stories, pain, expectations, and projections.

When emotional capacity is not replenished, processed, or structurally supported, even the most gifted individuals become vulnerable to despair, not because life lacks value, but because the system carrying that value has been depleted.

This does not excuse harm. But it does explain it.

As visibility increases, a new kind of pressure emerges, one that many leaders are never prepared to carry.

This helps explain why some high-profile public figures turn to substances, not necessarily because they desire addiction, but because they gained visibility before building the mental and emotional capacity required to sustain public life. Public exposure introduces relentless demand: constant scrutiny, loss of privacy, emotional exposure, performance expectations, and the weight of being projected upon by countless people. When internal regulation is insufficient, individuals often reach for external regulators, something to numb, slow, heighten, or stabilize what their internal systems cannot manage on their own.

In this context, substance use is frequently less about indulgence and more about self-medication for unmanaged pressure.

This framing does not excuse destructive behavior, nor does it romanticize addiction. It clarifies the sequence. Capacity failure under sustained visibility often precedes coping failure. The tragedy is not that success arrived; it is that success arrived before the internal systems were prepared to carry it.

Capacity does not automatically grow with influence. In many cases, influence accelerates exposure faster than emotional regulation, boundaries, and recovery rhythms can adapt. Without intentional capacity building—internal stability, support structures, and disciplined containment, visibility becomes destabilizing rather than empowering.

This is why capacity must be built before scale, not after it.

How Mental & Emotional Capacity Failure Shows Up

Mental and emotional capacity often collapses subtly before it collapses visibly.

Common indicators include:

i.   Chronic overthinking

ii. Avoidance of conflict disguised as wisdom

iii. Emotional numbness or volatility

iv. Defensiveness framed as discernment

v.   Mental replay of conversations

vi. Inability to disengage from problems after hours.

These are not personality flaws. They are capacity signals.

Unprocessed emotional load accumulates. Eventually, leaders respond not to the present moment, but to everything unresolved behind it.

Experience as a Capacity Constraint

Past trauma, betrayal, failure, abuse of authority, or incarceration can condition internal narratives that restrict capacity long after circumstances change.

Patterns that once protected survival, hyper-vigilance, mistrust, control, can later sabotage leadership. Capacity building requires recognizing when old strategies no longer serve new assignments.

Capacity does not grow by denial. It grows by awareness and regulation.

Why Mental & Emotional Capacity Must Precede Collaboration

Without mental and emotional capacity, collaboration becomes impossible.

Unregulated leaders misinterpret feedback, personalize disagreement, distrust motives, and control outcomes. Teams become unsafe, not because of intent, but because of instability.

This is why collaboration is addressed later in the book—after this dimension is established.

Rebuilding Mental & Emotional Capacity

Mental and emotional capacity grows through:

i. Awareness of internal patterns,

ii. Intentional emotional processing,

iii. Disciplined reflection,

iv. Reduced decision fatigue,

v. And regulated exposure to complexity.

It does not grow through avoidance or denial. It grows when leaders are willing to govern themselves before governing others.

Once leaders can regulate themselves internally, leadership moves into a new terrain. Responsibility is no longer only about pressure or emotion, it becomes about people: their differences, motivations, personalities, and trust dynamics.

This brings us to the third dimension of capacity:

Dimension Three: Relational Capacity (Discernment, Trust, and Shared Strength)

If mental and emotional capacity governs the leader internally, relational capacity determines whether leadership can multiply externally.

This is the dimension where many capable leaders quietly stall, not because they lack vision, discipline, or intelligence, but because leadership eventually demands what no individual can supply alone.

Relational capacity answers a decisive question: *Can the leader work effectively with others who are different, difficult, or more gifted in specific areas, without needing control, duplication, or emotional safety at all times?*

Historically, this has been my greatest area of deficiency.

Not because I disliked people, but because past betrayal, a perfectionistic mindset, and a deep sense of responsibility shaped how I related to others. I carried an internal narrative, often unspoken, that if something was going to be done well, it had to be done my way or at least done by someone who could duplicate my results or a better outcome.

That mindset produced outcomes, but it restricted scale.

Why Relational Capacity Is Often Underdeveloped

Relational capacity is frequently underdeveloped in high performers for one simple reason: competence masks deficiency.

When a leader is capable, intelligent, and results-driven, systems often compensate for relational gaps. Performance fills the silence. Outcomes excuse friction. Productivity delays the reckoning.

But capacity cannot be outsourced indefinitely.

Eventually, leadership reaches a level where:

i.   Results depend on people

ii. Systems outgrow personal oversight

iii. And outcomes require shared ownership.

This is where relational capacity becomes non-negotiable.

The Cost of Betrayal and the Birth of Rigidity

Betrayal does not only wound trust. It reshapes expectation.

Leaders who have been betrayed often respond by:

i.   Tightening control,

ii. Raising standards beyond realism

iii. Narrowing access

iv. And equating independence with safety.

Perfectionism often grows here—not as arrogance, but as self-protection.

The internal logic is subtle but powerful: If I can do it better, I don't have to depend on anyone.

This mindset produces reliability, but it suffocates collaboration.

Relational capacity cannot grow where self-protection masquerades as excellence.

When Results Expose Relational Gaps

For me, the turning point did not come through theory or reflection. It came through metrics.

My retention numbers were negative.

People were leaving, consistently.

To be clear, the decisions were logical. They were ethical. They were defensible.

Every termination had a reason. Every dismissal could be explained. From a performance standpoint, nothing I did was irrational. But leadership maturity begins when the question is no longer "Was I right?" but "What pattern is forming?"

I remember a one-on-one conversation with my supervisor that marked a quiet shift in my leadership journey.

She was not judgmental. She did not dispute that there were legitimate issues with the people who had been let go. She did not minimize the challenges.

Instead, she asked a single question that cut through everything:

"Who hired them?"

That question reframed the entire narrative.

It moved the conversation away from fault-finding and toward ownership. It forced me to see that while individuals may underperform, patterns belong to leaders. When the same outcome repeats, capacity, not circumstance, must be examined.

At that moment, leadership was no longer being evaluated solely by output. It was being evaluated by people.

Retention became a metric.

And with that shift, success could no longer be defined only by results delivered. I had to confront how people experienced leadership. The question changed from:

"Did we succeed?" to "Did people stay?"

That question was uncomfortable, but necessary.

Learning People Is a Leadership Skill

Up to that point, my leadership strength had been execution. I expected others to duplicate my standards, my pace, my precision. I assumed that clarity and competence should be enough.

It wasn't.

What I had not yet developed was relational discernment, the ability to recognize that excellence does not look the same in every personality, temperament, or processing style. **I was unconsciously building teams in my own image, rather than building vessels capable of holding what the work required.**

When I later encountered the book *Surrounded by Idiots* (often known by its earlier title *Surrounded by Fools*), all I could do was laugh at my former self. Not because I was foolish, but because I had been unaware.

I had been leading with competence, but without relational translation.

Relational capacity is complex. You cannot build relational capacity for eight billion people. You cannot become fluent in every personality type. But you can build enough awareness to stop demanding sameness where complementarity is required.

That realization changed how I hired. How I delegated. How I measured leadership success.

From Solo Excellence to Shared Capacity

My journey of learning, unlearning, and relearning relationships eventually gave birth to my first book on leadership. That work was not theoretical. It was born from lived tension—the realization that no matter how gifted you are, very little of lasting value is accomplished alone.

Relational capacity is not about liking everyone. It is about working effectively with difference.

It is the discipline of recognizing where your way is not the only way, releasing the need for replication, and building structures where diverse strengths can coexist without constant friction.

This is where many leaders stall, not because they lack vision or intelligence, but because they refuse to adjust how leadership is experienced by others.

Performance can carry you far. Relational capacity determines how long you last.

The Myth of Being the Brightest in the Room

One of the most dangerous illusions leaders carry is the belief that their intelligence entitles them to centrality.

No leader is ever the most brilliant in every room, nor should they be.

Your brilliance is limited by your ability. Your scale is determined by your relationships.

Growth requires proximity to minds that think differently, challenge assumptions, and operate in domains you do not master. Some of those minds may be abrasive. Some may be arrogant. Some may lack emotional polish.

But they often hold keys you do not have.

Relational capacity determines whether a leader can access those keys without being threatened by difference.

Why Duplication Is Not the Goal

One of the clearest illustrations of relational capacity comes from the story of the woman whose financial crisis was resolved not by increasing what she already had, but by expanding what could hold it.

The central issue was never the oil. She already had oil.

The solution was not more oil, better oil, or duplicated oil. The solution was vessels.

Her breakthrough did not come from producing more substance, but from increasing her capacity to contain, distribute, and steward what already existed. The oil only flowed to the extent that vessels were available. When the vessels stopped, the flow stopped, not because the oil was exhausted, but because capacity had reached its limit.

This is a relational principle, not merely a material one.

Many leaders assume that growth requires duplicating themselves, finding people who think like them, work like them, communicate like them, and validate their approach. This feels efficient, but it is fragile. It mistakes sameness for strength and control for capacity.

Duplication limits diversity. Diversity increases resilience.

Leadership does not scale through cloning. It scales through complementarity.

Relational capacity is the ability to recognize that what you carry does not need replication, it needs containment.

The woman did not need more oil. She needed more vessels.

Likewise, leaders do not need more brilliance, more ideas, or more personal output. What they need are people, systems, relationships, and partnerships, that can hold, carry, refine, and distribute what they already bring.

Complementarity Over Sameness

Relational capacity allows leaders to work effectively with people who: do not share their temperament, do not process information the same way, do not communicate identically, and do not prioritize the same details.

Some of these people may appear difficult. Some may seem arrogant, slow, unconventional, or misaligned at first glance.

But they often hold keys to the next level, keys the leader does not possess and cannot manufacture alone.

The goal is not sameness. The goal is synergy.

Synergy is not agreement. It is alignment of difference toward a shared outcome.

Why Leaders Resist Vessels

Leaders resist vessels for understandable reasons: vessels introduce dependence, vessels require trust, vessels reduce control, vessels expose limitation.

But refusing vessels does not preserve strength, it caps flow.

Oil stored in isolation stagnates. Oil released into vessels multiplies impact.

Relational capacity grows when leaders stop asking,
"Who can do this like me?"

and start asking,
"Who can hold what I carry in ways I cannot?"

The Relational Cost of Control

Control often masquerades as excellence.

Leaders who have been betrayed, disappointed, or let down may unconsciously decide that containment is safer than collaboration. But containment limits expansion. It forces the leader to become both the source and the vessel, an unsustainable arrangement.

No matter how gifted, no leader is designed to be both.

Relational capacity is what allows leaders to release flow without losing stewardship.

From Oil to Overflow

The oil was always sufficient. The flow was never the issue. The limit was relational capacity.

This is why relational capacity determines whether leadership plateaus or multiplies. It explains why some leaders burn out despite abundance, while others scale with grace despite constraint.

When leaders build vessels, healthy relationships, diverse teams, trusted partnerships, the oil they already carry finds room to move.

And when relational capacity expands, overflow becomes possible, not by force, but by design.

Discernment: The Core Skill of Relational Capacity

Relational capacity is not blind trust. It is discernment.

Discernment allows leaders to recognize strengths without ignoring risk, differentiate between character and competence, assign responsibility appropriately, and build teams that balance capability with integrity.

Leaders with low relational capacity either trust too quickly or not at all. Leaders with developed relational capacity trust wisely.

Discernment is what allows collaboration without chaos.

Diversity, Inclusion, and the Cost of Leading People

True leadership inevitably involves diversity of personality, perspective, culture, temperament, and skill.

Diversity complicates leadership. It slows consensus. It increases tension.

But it also expands capacity.

Leaders who avoid diversity do not avoid conflict, they avoid growth.

One of the most profound leadership models of relational capacity is seen in the way Jesus built his team, not through uniformity, but through intentional diversity. He worked with individuals of differing temperaments, backgrounds, maturity levels, and motives. He did not demand duplication. He cultivated development.

He led people as they were, without lowering the mission.

Relational capacity is the ability to hold people in process without losing direction.

Why Collaboration Feels Risky—but Is Essential

Collaboration requires vulnerability.

It requires leaders to:

i. Admit limitation,

ii. Release control

iii. And accept interdependence.

For leaders shaped by betrayal or failure, this feels dangerous.

But leadership without collaboration becomes isolation.

Relational capacity is what allows leaders to share load without losing authority.

Common Signs of Relational Capacity Failure

Relational capacity gaps often appear as:

i. Micromanagement

ii. High turnover,

iii. Conflict avoidance or escalation,

iv. Emotional distance,

v. Reliance on a few "safe" people,

vi. Or chronic disappointment with others.

These are not signs of bad leadership. They are signs of unresolved relational strain.

Building Relational Capacity Intentionally

Relational capacity grows when leaders:

i. Confront trust wounds honestly

ii. Release the need for duplication

iii. Learn personality differences

iv. Value contribution over conformity and build systems that protect both people and purpose.

It is slow work. It is humbling work. It is essential work.

Why This Dimension Unlocks Scale

No vision scales without people. No system survives without trust. No legacy endures without succession.

Relational capacity is what moves leadership from performance to perpetuation.

It is the bridge between individual effectiveness and collective impact.

Transition to the Next Dimension

Even the healthiest relationships cannot compensate for weak structure.

When roles are unclear, authority is undefined, and governance is absent, relational strength becomes strained. People carry what systems should hold.

This leads us to the fourth dimension of capacity: Structural Capacity—where systems, roles, and governance determine whether leadership stabilizes or fragments.

Structural capacity must always be examined alongside ethical capacity, because what you build will outlive you, and what it carries will shape lives you will never meet.

CHAPTER 6

◆————————————◆

Five Dimensions of Capacity Part II

▬▬▬

C apacity without ethics does not just fail, it institutionalizes damage.

Leadership does not end with the leader. What ultimately shapes outcomes across generations is not intention, brilliance, or even morality in isolation, but structure.

Part I of this framework focused on the capacities that reside within the individual: stamina, regulation, and relational intelligence. Those determine how much a person can carry. Part II shifts the focus outward, to what is built, governed, preserved, and transferred beyond the individual.

This is where capacity becomes historical.

Two dimensions dominate this territory: Structural Capacity and Ethical Capacity

Together, they determine whether success endures or decays, whether power heals or harms, and whether legacy uplifts or deforms.

Dimension Four: Structural Capacity When Design Determines Destiny

Structural capacity is the ability of systems to carry outcomes independent of individual effort. It is the most misunderstood and least discussed dimension of leadership capacity, yet it is the one that determines whether progress endures or collapses. Structural capacity answers questions that personal excellence cannot resolve:

i.   Can this organization function without constant heroics?

ii. Can outcomes be sustained when the founder steps away?

iii. Can growth occur without distortion, exploitation, or burnout?

iv. Can values survive scale?

Where personal and relational capacity focus on who the leader is, structural capacity focuses on what the leader builds.

Why Strong People Fail in Weak Structures

One of the great leadership myths is that exceptional individuals can compensate indefinitely for poor systems. They cannot.

Where structure is weak:

i.   Leaders absorb strain personally

ii.   Effort replaces design

iii. Urgency replaces rhythm

iv. Charisma replaces governance.

This works temporarily. It always fails eventually.

Strong individuals often burn out not because they lack stamina, but because they are carrying what should have been distributed structurally. Over time, the leader becomes the system. And when the leader falters, everything falters with them.

Structural capacity exists to prevent that collapse.

Structure Is the Silent Leader

Structure governs behavior more consistently than vision statements or values posters.

It determines:

i.   How decisions are made

ii. How conflict is resolved

iii. How accountability functions

iv. How power is transferred

v.   How continuity is preserved.

This is why leadership does not truly end with the leader. What matters most is not what a leader accomplishes, but what continues functioning when the leader is no longer present.

Structure is leadership extended through time.

Capacity Is Moral Neutral—Structure Is Not

One of the most sobering truths about structural capacity is this:

Capacity does not evaluate what it carries. It multiplies it.

This is why structure is never neutral in effect, even when it is neutral in intent. Systems amplify whatever values, assumptions, and hierarchies are embedded within them, whether noble or destructive.

History offers clear evidence.

The Greek Contribution: Capacity without Ethical Constraint

Ancient Greece is often celebrated as the birthplace of Western civilization, and that recognition is not misplaced. Greek society produced some of the earliest documented and systematized frameworks for human thought and organization. Among their enduring contributions were formal philosophy and logical reasoning, early scientific inquiry and observation, mathematics and geometry, political theory and civic organization, literature, rhetoric, and education.

What made these contributions powerful was not merely their originality, but their structure. These ideas were not left as isolated insights or individual brilliance. They were codified, taught, debated, preserved, and reproduced. They became part of an intellectual system designed to endure beyond the lifetime of any single thinker.

This is the essence of structural capacity.

I have been to Greece twice. Walking through its ruins—its academies, amphitheaters, and civic spaces—you cannot escape the sense of permanence. These were not accidental achievements. They were built with continuity in mind. And they worked. Greek thought continues to influence modern education, science, governance, and philosophy thousands of years later.

However, embedded within this extraordinary structural capacity was a profound ethical limitation—one that is often glossed over or left unexplained in general education.

How Hierarchies Were Embedded Into Thought Systems

Greek society did not merely practice inequality; it theorized it.

Certain groups of people were classified as inherently lesser, not always by naming skin color explicitly, but by describing physical features, geographic origin, and supposed intellectual or moral capacity. These descriptions were often presented as observations rather than opinions, which made them persuasive, especially when coming from thinkers who had already demonstrated brilliance in other domains.

This is a critical point.

When people with documented success in science, philosophy, and governance articulate ideas about human hierarchy, those ideas carry disproportionate credibility. They are more likely to be accepted uncritically by later generations, especially by those who have not studied the full historical context.

In Greek writings, people from certain regions—particularly parts of Africa and other conquered territories—were described in ways that implied inferiority, primitiveness, or suitability for servitude. The language was often indirect, framed as natural order rather than explicit prejudice. But the implication was clear: not all humans were regarded as equally human.

Slavery, therefore, was not simply an economic practice. It was intellectually justified.

It was explained. It was normalized. It was embedded into social, political, and philosophical systems.

This distinction matters.

Practices can fade. Systems endure.

Why This Is a Capacity Issue, Not a Cultural Critique

The importance of this history lies not in assigning modern moral judgment to ancient societies, but in understanding a capacity principle:

> *Structural capacity amplifies whatever values are embedded within it.*

Greek society built extraordinary systems for preserving and transmitting knowledge. But those same systems also preserved distorted assumptions about human worth. When the Roman Empire later absorbed Greek philosophy, education, and governance structures, it also absorbed these classifications.

Over time, these ideas traveled, through empires, laws, economic models, and social norms, often stripped of their original context, but still carrying their underlying assumptions. Many people who later adopted these frameworks had never studied their origins. They trusted the authority of the system because it came from civilizations known for brilliance and achievement.

This is how flawed ideas become durable.

Not because everyone agrees with them consciously, but because they are carried by structures that work in other areas.

The architects died. The systems remained. The influence endured.

This is the weight, and the danger, of structural capacity.

Structure Outlives Intention

One of the most common leadership misconceptions is the belief that good intentions are sufficient to protect outcomes. History consistently disproves this assumption.

Intentions are personal. Structures are impersonal.

Intentions fade with time, leadership change, and shifting priorities. Structures persist. They continue to shape behavior, distribute power, and define norms long after the original intent is forgotten.

This is why systems-built centuries ago can still influence modern realities, financial, social, and institutional, even when their creators are long gone.

Financial Architecture as Structural Capacity When Systems Operate Beyond Visibility

One of the clearest modern examples of structural capacity can be found in global financial architecture.

In the early twentieth century, a small group of financial leaders met privately at Jekyll Island to design a new banking framework for the United States. The goal was not simply to address immediate economic instability, but to create a system capable of stabilizing financial operations independent of day-to-day political control.

What emerged from those conversations was not a temporary policy, but an enduring structure, one that would outlive its architects and operate largely outside public awareness. This episode and its long-term implications have been examined extensively by historians and critics, including G. Edward Griffin in *The Creature from Jekyll Island.*

The financial frameworks designed during that period still shape global economic systems today.

Most people affected by these systems have never heard of the meeting, the individuals involved, or the motivations behind the design. Yet their daily lives, interest rates, access to credit, inflation, savings protection, and economic cycles are influenced by decisions embedded into structures created over a century ago.

This is structural capacity at work.

Why Financial Structures Endure

Financial systems are among the most powerful examples of capacity because they are designed to function across generations, across administrations, across economic cycles, across public opinion.

They do not rely on personality, popularity, or visibility. They rely on architecture.

Institutions such as central banking mechanisms and deposit insurance frameworks were designed to absorb shocks, regulate behavior, and maintain continuity even when leadership changes or public trust fluctuates.

For example, the creation of deposit insurance mechanisms fundamentally altered how risk is distributed within the banking system. While the stated goal was stability and public confidence, the deeper capacity principle was this:

Risk was no longer borne solely by individuals or individual institutions but redistributed across a system.

Whether one views these outcomes as beneficial, flawed, or mixed is not the point here. The leadership lesson lies in how effectively structure carries consequence.

Structure Does Not Ask Permission

Financial structures do not require public understanding to function. They do not need agreement. They do not need explanation to those affected by them.

They operate because:

i. The rules are embedded

ii. Participation is assumed

iii. Alternatives are limited

iv. And continuity is enforced structurally rather than emotionally.

This is why financial systems can influence billions of lives with minimal public awareness. Not because people are uninformed, but because structure does not depend on consent once adopted.

This is a sobering leadership truth.

The Capacity Lesson for Leaders

What financial architecture demonstrates clearly is this:

When systems are well-designed, they do not need constant reinforcement. When systems are poorly designed, they require constant intervention.

Leaders often underestimate the power of structure because it is invisible once established. Attention is drawn to personalities, policies, and crises, while the architecture quietly governs outcomes in the background.

This is why leaders who focus only on vision, intention, or charisma often fail to produce lasting impact. Without structural capacity, influence evaporates when attention shifts.

Independence from Intent

One of the defining characteristics of strong structural capacity is independence from original intent.

The designers of financial frameworks may have had specific goals, concerns, or assumptions. Over time, circumstances change, leadership changes, and societal values evolve. Yet the system continues to operate according to its original architecture.

This is neither inherently good nor inherently bad.

It is simply how capacity works.

Once built, structure carries forward what was embedded within it, efficiently, relentlessly, and often without reflection.

Why This Matters Beyond Finance

The financial example is instructive not because every leader is building a banking system, but because every leader is building something that will eventually operate without them:

i.   Organizations

ii. Policies

iii. Cultures

iv. Workflows

v.   Governance models.

The question is not whether those systems will endure. The question is what they will preserve.

Structural Capacity as Leadership Responsibility

Structural capacity places a unique responsibility on leaders: to think beyond outcomes and consider consequences over time.

It forces leaders to ask:

i.   Who benefits from this structure?

ii. Who bears the cost?

iii. What behaviors does it reward?

iv. What behaviors does it normalize?

v.   What happens when intentions are forgotten?

Financial systems remind us that once structure is in place, it becomes exceedingly difficult to reverse—even when its impact is widely felt.

That is why structural capacity must be built with foresight, restraint, and ethical awareness.

Financial architecture demonstrates a principle every leader must confront:

> **What you build will eventually lead without you. And when it does, it will not ask what you intended, it will do what it was designed to do.**

This is the true weight of structural capacity.

And yet, the structure persists.

This is not an argument against structure. It is a warning about building structure without ethical capacity.

The Leadership Implication

Structural capacity is not optional for leaders who intend to build something that lasts. But it is also not sufficient on its own.

When ethics lag capacity:

i. Harm becomes scalable

ii. Injustice becomes normalized

iii. Distortion becomes institutionalized.

This is why leaders must ask not only Can this system endure? but also What exactly is it preserving?

Capacity does not discriminate. It multiplies.

That is why *structural capacity must always be examined alongside ethical capacity, because what you build will outlive you, and what it carries will shape lives you will never meet.*

Legacy is not accidental. It is engineered.

Why Some Nations Stall While Others Multiply Talent

Structural capacity also explains a modern phenomenon many observe but struggle to articulate.

Why do individuals from underdeveloped or unstable nations often excel when they migrate to countries with stronger systems?

The answer is not intelligence. It is not work ethic. It is not suddenly acquired discipline.

It is structure.

When people move from environments where systems are unreliable to environments where:

i. Rules are predictable

ii. Processes are enforced

iii. Accountability is institutional,

iv. Effort is rewarded consistently; their latent capacity is finally able to express itself.

Where structure is weak, people compensate with extraordinary effort just to survive. Where structure is strong, effort is freed for creativity, innovation, and growth.

This is not a judgment of people. It is a diagnosis of systems.

Structural Capacity in Leadership Contexts

In organizations, structural capacity shows up in:

i. Clear roles and decision rights

ii. Functional delegation,

iii. Repeatable processes,

iv. Governance mechanisms,

v. Succession planning

vi. Institutional memory.

Without these, leaders become bottlenecks. Decisions slow. Conflict escalates. Everything requires approval. The organization functions—but only at the cost of exhaustion.

With structural capacity:

i. Authority is distributed

ii. Accountability is shared

iii. Continuity is protected

iv. Leaders are freed to think rather than constantly react.

Structure does not replace leadership. It preserves it.

The Cost of Neglecting Structure

Leaders who ignore structural capacity often experience:

i. Chronic urgency,

ii. Decision fatigue

iii. Emotional overload

iv. Ethical drift

v. Inability to scale

vi. Fragility masked as momentum.

These are not personality flaws. They are structural failures.

When systems cannot carry weight, people are forced to absorb it. Over time, even the strongest individual fracture.

Structural capacity is the bridge between vision and longevity.

Vision without structure creates enthusiasm. Structure without vision creates bureaucracy. But vision supported by structure creates endurance.

This is why structural capacity is not optional for leaders who intend to last. It is not administrative overhead. It is leadership foresight.

What you build will eventually lead without you.

The only question is: What values will it carry when you are no longer there to correct it?

Structural Capacity Is Stewardship across Time

To build structural capacity is to think beyond your tenure, your reputation, and your immediate success. It is to ask:

i. What happens after me?

ii. What survives pressure?

iii. What resists corruption?

iv. What continues functioning when personalities change?

This is the difference between influence and legacy.

Structural capacity ensures that what is good does not depend on who is present to enforce it.

Personal capacity may get you started. Relational capacity may help you grow. But only structural capacity determines whether what you build will endure.

This is why civilizations rise and fall. This is why organizations flourish or fracture. This is why leaders are remembered or forgotten.

Capacity becomes history when it is embedded in structure

Dimension Five: Ethical Capacity the Ability to Carry Power without Corruption

Ethical capacity is the ability to hold power, influence, responsibility, and autonomy without moral erosion.

It is not about perfection. It is not about public image. It is not about adherence to stated values when they are convenient.

Ethical capacity answers a far more demanding question:

Can this leader remain aligned when restraint is no longer enforced externally?

Many leaders assume ethics are static—that once values are established, they will automatically guide behavior at higher levels. History and experience prove otherwise. Ethics are not fixed traits; they are capacities that must grow alongside power.

When ethical capacity does not expand at the same rate as authority, corruption is not a possibility, it is an inevitability.

Why Ethical Failure Is Rarely Sudden

Ethical collapse almost never begins with obvious wrongdoing. It begins quietly, incrementally, and often invisibly.

It starts with:

i.   Justified exceptions,

ii. Small shortcuts,

iii. Selective enforcement of rules

iv. Rationalized compromises

v. Silence where correction is required.

Each step feels minor. Each decision seems reasonable in isolation. But over time, the accumulation of unchallenged exceptions reshapes what feels normal.

This is why ethical failure often surprises observers but rarely surprises those closest to the system. The drift was gradual. The warning signs were present. But capacity to resist was insufficient.

Ethical capacity determines whether a leader can withstand prolonged exposure to power without internal distortion.

Power Changes the Moral Environment

One of the most misunderstood realities of leadership is that power alters the ethical landscape.

As authority increases:

i.   Consequences are delayed

ii. Oversight decreases

iii. Access expands

iv. Alternatives narrow

v.   Dissent becomes riskier for others.

This creates a moral asymmetry. Leaders are increasingly insulated from the immediate feedback that once shaped their behavior. What would have been corrected early at lower levels now persists unchallenged.

Ethical capacity is the ability to remain accountable when accountability is no longer enforced.

Why Intentions Are Insufficient

Many leaders rely on good intentions as a safeguard. They believe that because they mean well, outcomes will remain aligned.

Intentions do not scale. Capacity does.

Ethical capacity must be designed, not assumed. It requires structures, practices, and internal disciplines that restrain behavior even when no one is watching—or willing to speak.

This is why ethics must be treated as a capacity issue, not a character slogan.

Ethical Capacity and Structural Capacity Are Interdependent

Structural capacity determines what lasts. Ethical capacity determines what lasts without harm.

History offers repeated examples of systems that were:

i. Efficient but exploitative

ii. Stable but dehumanizing

iii. Orderly but unjust.

These systems did not fail structurally. They failed ethically.

And because the structures were strong, the harm was durable.

This is the sobering truth:

When ethical capacity lags structural capacity, damage becomes institutional.

The Cost of Ethical Underdevelopment

Leaders with insufficient ethical capacity often exhibit recognizable patterns:

i.   Justification of harm as "necessary"

ii. Silencing of dissent in the name of unity

iii. Selective application of standards

iv. Erosion of transparency

v.   Increasing isolation from corrective voices.

These behaviors are rarely experienced by the leader as corruption. They are experienced as pressure, necessity, or responsibility.

Ethical failure does not feel unethical to the person committing it. It feels justified.

This is why ethical capacity must be built before power expands, not after damage occurs.

Ethical Capacity Is About Restraint, Not Control

True ethical strength is not demonstrated by the ability to enforce rules on others, but by the ability to restrain oneself.

It is the capacity to:

i. Say no when saying yes would benefit you

ii. Slow down when speed would conceal flaws

iii. Remain transparent when opacity would protect reputation

iv. Submit to correction when authority would silence it.

Ethical capacity is quiet. It does not announce itself. But it governs everything beneath the surface.

Ethical Capacity and Longevity

Leaders often ask how to build legacy. The unspoken assumption is that legacy is created through impact, scale, or recognition.

But legacy is ultimately shaped by what survives scrutiny over time.

Ethical capacity determines whether:

i.   Achievements remain admirable,

ii. Systems retain trust

iii. Influence endures without reinterpretation

iv. Successors inherit strength rather than damage.

Many leaders are remembered not for what they built, but for what had to be dismantled after them.

That is not a failure of intelligence or vision. It is a failure of ethical capacity.

Ethical Capacity as Stewardship

Ethical leadership is stewardship across time.

It recognizes that:

i.   Power is borrowed

ii. Authority is temporary

iii. Impact extends beyond intent

iv. Decisions echo beyond tenure.

Ethical capacity allows leaders to act with awareness of those realities, not fearfully, but responsibly.

A Diagnostic Question for Leaders

A simple way to assess ethical capacity is to ask: What behaviors does my position allow me to get away with? What feedback am I no longer hearing? What decisions would I make differently if consequences were immediate? Who can confront me without fear?

The answers to these questions reveal far more than any stated value system.

Ethical capacity is not about being good. It is about being governed when no one else is governing you.

Structural capacity ensures that what you build will last. Ethical capacity ensures that what lasts will not destroy.

Together, they determine whether leadership becomes legacy or cautionary tale.

The Capacity Diagnostic a Five-Dimension Self-Assessment Tool

Purpose of This Assessment

This assessment is designed to help leaders identify where capacity is strong, where it is strained, and where it is underdeveloped across five critical dimensions. It is not a personality test, nor a measure of talent or intelligence. It is a structural assessment of sustainability.

The goal is clarity, not judgment.

Capacity gaps do not indicate failure. They indicate where reinforcement is required before expansion continues.

How to Use This Tool

For each statement, rate yourself on a scale of 1 to 5:

1. Strongly Disagree

2. Disagree

3. Neutral / Inconsistent

4. Agree

5. Strongly Agree

Answer based on patterns over time, not isolated moments.

Dimension One: Personal Capacity (Stamina, health, boundaries, pace)

1. I can sustain my current level of responsibility without chronic exhaustion.

2. My schedule reflects intentional rest, not just recovery from burnout.

3. I maintain clear boundaries around time, energy, and access.

4. My physical health supports, not undermines my leadership demands.

5. I can slow down without guilt when reinforcement is needed.

Score Interpretation

20 to 25: Sustainable personal capacity

13 to 19: Functional but strained

Below 13: Capacity deficit requiring immediate attention

Dimension Two: Mental & Emotional Capacity (Regulation, mindset, pressure tolerance)

1. I can receive criticism without becoming defensive or reactive.

2. I do not take disagreement or resistance personally.

3. I remain emotionally steady under prolonged pressure.

4. I am aware of how past experiences influence my current reactions.

5. I can hold complexity and ambiguity without forcing premature closure.

Score Interpretation

20–25: High emotional regulation

13–19: Situational stability

Below 13: Emotional load exceeding capacity

Dimension Three: Relational Capacity (Trust, collaboration, discernment, people leadership)

1. I can work effectively with people who think and operate differently from me.

2. I do not require others to duplicate my style to earn my trust.

3. I delegate authority without excessive monitoring or control.

4. I repair relational strain promptly rather than avoiding it.

5. I value complementarity over sameness in teams.

Score Interpretation

> 20–25: Scalable relational capacity
>
> 13–19: Selective collaboration
>
> Below 13: Relational bottleneck risk

Dimension Four: Structural Capacity (Systems, governance, continuity)

1. Outcomes in my leadership context do not depend solely on my presence.

2. Roles, processes, and decision rights are clearly defined.

3. Authority and accountability are distributed, not centralized.

4. Systems function without constant intervention or heroics.

5. There is a plan for continuity beyond my tenure.

Score Interpretation

> 20–25: Durable structural capacity
>
> 13–19: Leader-dependent systems
>
> Below 13: Structural fragility

Dimension Five: Ethical Capacity (Integrity under power, restraint, moral stamina)

1. I maintain accountability even when oversight is minimal.

2. I resist justifying unethical shortcuts under pressure.

3. I welcome correction from people with less positional power.

4. My decisions remain consistent regardless of visibility or consequence.

5. I have safeguards that restrain me when power increases.

Score Interpretation

20–25: Strong ethical resilience

13–19: Context-dependent ethics

Below 13: Ethical risk zone

Reading the Results

High scores across all five dimensions indicate balanced capacity and readiness for sustained responsibility.

Uneven scores explain why success may be replicable in some areas but fragile in others.

Low scores in any dimension signal a need for reinforcement before expansion.

Capacity does not fail where effort is lacking. It fails where structure is insufficient.

Important Insight

Capacity is domain specific. A leader may score high in personal and ethical capacity yet remain constrained by relational or structural limitations. The goal is not uniform excellence, but intentional alignment.

Next Step Reflection

After completing this assessment, ask:

i. Which dimension is currently carrying the most strain?

ii. What expansion am I pursuing that my capacity may not yet support?

iii. What must be strengthened before I grow further?

Capacity is not built by denial or acceleration. It is built by honest diagnosis followed by deliberate design.

*Those who accomplished extraordinary
things in the past did not arrive fully
formed. They built capacity deliberately,
step by step, often in obscurity long before
their impact became visible.*

Dr. Joke Solanke

CHAPTER 7

◆———————————◆

The Myth of More: Why Growth Alone Solves Nothing

———

E xpansion without capacity is acceleration toward failure.

Growth is one of the most celebrated concepts in modern leadership. We are taught to pursue it relentlessly—grow the organization, grow the influence, grow the platform, grow the revenue, grow the audience. Growth is framed as progress, expansion as success, and increase as evidence that something is working.

But growth is not neutral.

Growth is an amplifier. It does not correct weakness, it exposes it. It does not stabilize dysfunction, it magnifies it. It does not heal fragility, it accelerates collapse.

One of the most dangerous assumptions leaders carry is the belief that more will fix what is already strained. More people. More money. More visibility. More opportunity. More authority. More reach.

This assumption is not only wrong, it is costly.

Growth does not solve structural weakness. It intensifies it.

The goal of this chapter is to dismantle the myth of more and replace it with a more sobering, but far more liberating truth: capacity must precede expansion, or expansion becomes the mechanism of failure.

Why Growth Feels Like the Answer

The appeal of growth is understandable. Growth feels active. It feels hopeful. It feels like movement. When something is not working, expansion offers the illusion of escape, if we just get bigger, faster, stronger, louder, or more resourced, the problems will resolve themselves.

Growth promises relief without introspection.

It allows leaders to avoid harder questions: Why is this system strained? Why is this leader exhausted? Why are results inconsistent? Why does success feel fragile?

Growth feels easier than restraint. Expansion feels more rewarding than assessment. Motion feels better than pause.

But leadership reality is unforgiving: what you do not confront before growth will confront you during growth.

Growth Magnifies Gaps

Growth does not create problems. It reveals the ones already present.

When capacity is insufficient:

i.   Growth magnifies inefficiency,

ii. Expansion intensifies misalignment

iii. Scale exposes relational fractures

iv. Visibility amplifies immaturity

v.   And authority tests integrity.

Small gaps are manageable at small scale. They become catastrophic at large scale.

A leader with poor emotional regulation may function well with a small team. At scale, that same emotional volatility becomes abuse, intimidation, or public scandal. A system with weak accountability may limp along when demand is low. Under growth, it collapses under its own weight. A culture built on heroics may look impressive early. Over time, it burns out its best people and normalizes dysfunction.

Growth does not ask permission before exposing these realities. It simply applies pressure until structure responds, or fails.

Money ≠ Stability

One of the most persistent myths in leadership is that financial increase automatically produces organizational stability.

It does not.

Money is a resource, not a regulator.

Without capacity:

i.   Money accelerates poor decisions

ii. Funding amplifies mismanagement

iii. Financial access multiplies ethical risk

iv. And abundance removes constraints that once forced discipline.

Many organizations fail not because they lacked resources, but because they received them too early. Sudden access to capital without governance often destabilizes rather than strengthens.

Money does not create discipline. It reveals whether discipline already exists.

Where structure is weak, money becomes fuel for chaos. Where systems are underdeveloped, resources overwhelm rather than empower.

This is why some organizations implode immediately after funding, while others stabilize and mature. The difference is not money. It is capacity.

People ≠ Strength

Another common illusion is that adding people automatically increases strength.

People do not increase capacity by default. They increase complexity.

Every additional person introduces:

i.   Communication load

ii. Emotional dynamics

iii. Decision pathways

iv. Accountability demands

v.   And relational responsibility.

Leaders who lack relational and structural capacity often interpret growth in headcount as relief; in reality, it becomes a multiplier of strain. Without clarity:

i.   People slow momentum

ii. Teams fragment

iii. Misalignment grows

iv. Conflict intensifies

v.   And leaders become bottlenecks.

This is why some leaders feel more overwhelmed as their teams grow, not less. They have expanded people without expanding governance.

People do not fix weak leadership. They expose it.

Visibility ≠ Authority

Visibility is often mistaken for authority. Influence for leadership. Platform for capacity.

Visibility amplifies voice, but it does not create weight-bearing ability.

A leader can be highly visible and deeply fragile. A platform can grow faster than the person standing on it. When this happens, pressure increases while internal structure remains unchanged.

This is why:

i. Some leaders collapse publicly

ii. Some movements fracture under scrutiny

iii. Some voices disintegrate under opposition

iv. And some platforms cannot survive criticism.

Visibility tests maturity. Authority requires capacity.

When visibility exceeds capacity, leaders become defensive, reactive, or controlling. They confuse disagreement with threat. They personalize critique. They collapse under pressure that capacity would have absorbed quietly.

Roots before Height

In nature, growth is never judged by height alone.

What determines longevity is what cannot be seen: the root system.

A tall tree with shallow roots is not impressive, it is dangerous. It becomes a liability the moment wind, rain, or resistance arrives.

Roots:

i. Distribute weight

ii. Absorb shock

iii. Stabilize growth

iv. And allow endurance across seasons.

Leadership capacity functions the same way. Roots are built underground, through discipline, structure, emotional maturity, relational discernment, ethical restraint, and systems thinking.

Growth without roots is not ambition. It is negligence.

Why Expansion Feels Like Progress (Even When It Isn't)

Expansion creates momentum. Momentum creates validation. Validation feels like success.

But momentum can exist without sustainability.

This is why leaders sometimes feel most confident just before collapse. Momentum masks structural strain. Applause quiets warning signals. Activity replaces assessment.

Capacity-building often feels slow and unimpressive. Growth feels exciting. But excitement does not predict endurance.

The discipline of leadership is learning to value stability over speed, structure over spectacle, and endurance over applause.

The Cost of Ignoring Capacity

When leaders prioritize growth over capacity, several patterns emerge:

i.   Chronic urgency becomes normal

ii. Leaders become perpetual problem-solvers

iii. Systems require constant intervention

iv. Emotional exhaustion is spiritualized or minimized

v. And collapse is explained as "burnout" rather than design failure.

These are not personal flaws. They are architectural consequences.

Expansion without capacity does not fail immediately. It fails eventually. And when it does, the cost is higher, because more people, resources, and responsibility are involved.

When Growth Exposes What Capacity Could Not Carry

Theory becomes trustworthy when readers recognize themselves in it. Capacity failure is rarely announced with drama; it is revealed through patterns leaders normalize because growth is still occurring.

The following illustrations are not anomalies. They are predictable outcomes when expansion outruns structure.

Case 1: The High-Growth Organization That Collapsed Under Success

The organization began with clarity. Its founding team was aligned, agile, and mission driven. Early growth was organic clients arrived through referrals, systems were informal but functional, and leadership was hands-on.

Then growth accelerated.

Revenue doubled. Headcount tripled. New markets opened. Externally, everything looked successful. Internally, pressure mounted.

Meetings multiplied, but decisions slowed. Roles overlapped, but accountability blurred. Leaders worked longer hours, but effectiveness declined.

Instead of pausing to strengthen structure, leadership responded with more growth: more hires to relieve workload, more managers to handle complexity, more initiatives to maintain momentum.

But capacity had not been built to govern scale.

Communication fractured. Middle managers lacked authority. Senior leaders became bottlenecks. The organization relied increasingly on heroic effort rather than systems.

Eventually: key leaders burned out, turnover increased, quality declined, trust eroded, and growth stalled.

The failure was not strategic. It was architectural.

The organization did not collapse because it grew. It collapsed because it grew without reinforcing capacity at each level.

Case 2: The Leader Who Became the Bottleneck

This leader was brilliant, decisive, and respected. In early stages, their personal involvement was an asset. They solved problems quickly, maintained quality, and protected standards.

As responsibility increased, their role should have shifted from executor to governor.

It did not.

Every decision still came through them. Every conflict required their intervention. Every exception needed their approval.

The organization continued to grow, but the leader did not redistribute authority.

At scale, what once looked like excellence became obstruction.

People waited. Decisions stalled. Innovation slowed. Frustration grew. Eventually, the leader felt overwhelmed and misunderstood.

From their perspective, they were carrying everything. From the system's perspective, they were blocking flow.

This is one of the clearest signs of capacity failure: when leadership strength becomes systemic weakness.

The issue was not ego. It was undeveloped capacity for delegation, governance, and shared authority.

Case 3: Emotional Volatility at Scale

At small scale, emotional reactions are often absorbed quietly. At large scale, they ripple.

In this case, a leader known for passion and intensity built a visible platform. Their message resonated. Their audience expanded. Their influence grew.

But emotional regulation did not evolve with visibility.

Under criticism, responses became defensive. Disagreement was interpreted as disloyalty. Stress was externalized through tone, public comments, and impulsive decisions.

What might have been overlooked in private settings became magnified publicly.

The leader had influence without emotional capacity at scale.

As pressure increased, so did volatility. The platform survived, but trust eroded. People stayed connected for content, not leadership.

This illustrates a hard truth: Emotional capacity that is sufficient at one level becomes insufficient at another.

Case 4: Systems That Require Heroics to Function

In many organizations, especially healthcare, nonprofit, and public service sectors, systems survive only because individuals compensate for structural weakness.

Staff work excessive hours. Leaders absorb emotional fallout. Informal workarounds replace formal processes.

At first, this looks admirable. Over time, it becomes dangerous.

When systems require constant heroics: burnout becomes normalized, errors increase, ethical shortcuts appear, and sustainability erodes.

The system does not fail immediately because people sacrifice themselves to keep it running.

But sacrifice is not capacity. It is substitution.

Eventually, the cost becomes unbearable.

Case 5: Success That Cannot Be Repeated

One of the clearest indicators of insufficient capacity is non-repeatable success.

A leader succeeds once—but cannot reproduce results elsewhere. An organization thrives briefly—but cannot stabilize gains. A system works under specific conditions—but collapses when variables change.

This is not bad luck.

It is evidence that outcomes exceeded structure.

Repeatability is the fingerprint of capacity. If success cannot be repeated, it was likely driven by: extraordinary effort, unique timing, singular personalities, or unsustainable pressure.

Capacity allows success to endure beyond favorable conditions.

Why These Failures Are Normalized

These patterns persist because growth masks fragility.

As long as outcomes appear positive, leaders rationalize strain: "This season is intense." "Once we hire more people, it will stabilize." "We just need more funding." "This is what leadership requires."

But these explanations delay necessary intervention.

Capacity failure rarely announces itself as failure. It announces itself as busyness, urgency, and overextension.

The Common Thread

Across all these cases, the issue is not intelligence, effort, or vision.

The issue is sequencing.

Growth came before capacity. Expansion preceded reinforcement. Visibility outpaced maturity.

And pressure revealed what preparation did not address.

Why This Matters

Leaders often ask how to avoid failure. The better question is how to recognize capacity strain before collapse.

Failure is not sudden. It is tolerated. It is normalized. It is explained away, until systems can no longer carry the weight.

Understanding these patterns restores agency. It allows leaders to intervene early. It reframes restraint as wisdom, not fear.

Preparing for the Next Layer

If capacity failure is predictable, then leadership demands a new skill: the ability to recognize strain patterns before damage occurs.

That is where we go next.

In the following chapter, we will examine how capacity failure shows up, not in theory, but in daily leadership behaviors, organizational rhythms, and system responses.

Because collapse does not begin with disaster. It begins with normalization.

And leaders who can see it early can redesign before it is too late.

Most leadership failures do not begin with scandal, incompetence, or rebellion. They begin quietly, with small accommodations and unexamined strain.

CHAPTER 8

◆————————————◆

How Capacity Failure Actually Shows Up

——

C apacity failure is rarely dramatic—it is normalized until collapse.

One of the most misunderstood aspects of leadership growth is the assumption that capacity automatically increases with promotion. It does not. Titles change faster than structures. Responsibility expands faster than readiness. Authority is often granted before the internal, relational, and systemic architecture required to sustain it has been built.

This misunderstanding explains why capable people fail at higher levels, why gifted leaders burn out, and why organizations recycle the same leadership problems under different names.

Capacity is not linear. It is contextual.

A person may demonstrate strong capacity in one domain and severe deficiency in another. They may function well at one level of responsibility and collapse at the next. This is not hypocrisy or inconsistency. It is a failure to rebuild capacity as responsibility changes.

Why Capacity Does Not Transfer Automatically

Performance earns visibility. Capacity determines sustainability.

In early stages of leadership, effort can compensate for weak structure. Hard work, intelligence, and personal discipline can mask capacity gaps for a season. But as responsibility increases, effort becomes insufficient. What once worked becomes a liability.

Each level of responsibility introduces new forms of weight:

i.   Greater consequence

ii. Longer time horizons

iii. Increased relational complexity

iv. Moral and ethical exposure

v.   And systemic impact.

When leaders attempt to carry new weight using old structures, strain follows. But strain is only the beginning. If the structure is not redesigned, pressure does not merely exhaust it, it ruptures it, often causing damage deeper than what is immediately visible.

Capacity must be intentionally rebuilt with promotion. Promotion elevates position and responsibility, but it does not automatically redesign structure or upgrade internal architecture. This is one of the costliest misunderstandings in leadership development. *Titles elevate visibility, authority, and expectation, but they do not rebuild the internal frameworks required to sustain what follows.* Responsibility increases faster than capacity unless capacity is intentionally redesigned.

When people are promoted, they often assume that access itself will generate growth—that exposure will somehow produce maturity, that authority will create clarity, and that experience will naturally refine judgment. Exposure without preparation accelerates breakdown. Authority without internal reconfiguration magnifies weakness. Experience without reflection reinforces blind spots.

Promotion does not upgrade:

i.   Emotional regulation,

ii. Decision-making frameworks,

iii. Ethical resilience,

iv. Relational discernment, or stamina for sustained pressure.

Those elements must be rebuilt deliberately.

What worked at the previous level often becomes insufficient, or even dangerous, at the next. Structures designed for one level of responsibility are not neutral when reused at another; they become limiting. When new weight is placed on old architecture, the result is not growth but distortion.

At first, the signs appear mild: longer hours, increased urgency, heightened stress, relational friction. Leaders often interpret these as normal growing pains. They push harder. They compensate with effort. They normalize overload.

But strain is only the early warning.

If the structure is not redesigned, pressure does not stretch it indefinitely, it ruptures it. And rupture does not simply exhaust the leader; it damages trust, systems, and people. In many cases, the harm outlives the leader's tenure.

This is why leadership failure so often surprises observers, but not those paying attention to structure. Collapse looks sudden only because the architectural mismatch was ignored for too long.

Capacity must be rebuilt before responsibility expands, not after failure exposes the gap.

Why Capacity Must Be Rebuilt in Phases

Capacity does not expand globally. It expands contextually.

Each new level of responsibility introduces different kinds of weight:

i. Cognitive weight (decision complexity)

ii. Emotional weight (relational tension)

iii. Ethical weight (moral consequence)

iv. And temporal weight (longer horizons of accountability).

Because the weight changes, the structure must change.

This is why leadership development that focuses only on skill enhancement repeatedly fails. Skills improve execution, but they do not redesign internal load-bearing systems. A leader can become more efficient and still be structurally unprepared for the responsibility they are stepping into.

Capacity rebuilding requires phases:

i. Recognition—acknowledging that the old structure is insufficient.

ii. Assessment—identifying where strain is already present.

iii. Redesign—strengthening internal, relational, and systemic supports.

iv. Stabilization—allowing the new structure to function under pressure.

v. Expansion—only then increasing responsibility.

Skipping these phases does not save time. It creates deferred failure.

Why This Must Be Understood Before Discussing Levels

Without this understanding, the level-by-level analysis that follows can be misread as a hierarchy of importance rather than a map of responsibility. The goal is not to imply that higher levels are "better," but to show that each level requires a different kind of capacity.

Many leaders are operating at levels for which they were never structurally prepared—not because they lack intelligence or commitment, but because no one taught them that capacity must evolve.

This is why:

i. Excellent individual contributors struggle as team leaders

ii. Strong team leaders' fracture at organizational levels

iii. And visionary leaders fail as system stewards.

The failure is not effort. It is architecture.

With this foundation in place, we can now examine capacity where it first becomes visible—at the level of individual responsibility.

Level One: Individual Contributor Capacity

At the individual contributor level, responsibility is primarily personal and task oriented. The scope of accountability is limited, visible, and largely controllable. Outcomes are closely tied to personal effort, competence, and discipline.

This level forms the entry point of capacity, and for many people it is where their strongest capabilities are expressed.

How Success Is Measured at This Level

Success at the individual contributor level is assessed through clear, tangible indicators:

i. Competence, the ability to perform assigned tasks correctly and efficiently

ii. Reliability—consistency in showing up and delivering as expected

iii. Consistency—stable output over time, not sporadic excellence

iv. Technical proficiency—mastery of the specific skills required for the role

v. Personal discipline—self-management, focus, and follow-through

At this level, effort produces visible results. Cause and effect are closely aligned. When something goes wrong, the source is often identifiable—and correctable through improved skill or discipline.

What Capacity Looks Like at the Individual Level

Capacity at this stage focuses on execution strength. It includes:

i. Skill acquisition - learning what the role requires and performing it with increasing competence

ii. Time management - prioritizing tasks, managing deadlines, and sequencing work effectively

iii. Boundary awareness - knowing limits, avoiding overextension, and managing energy responsibly

iv. Personal stamina - the ability to sustain performance without chronic exhaustion

v. Execution quality - attention to detail, accuracy, and consistency in output

At this level, capacity is largely internal. The individual is responsible for managing performance, pace, and resilience. Systems and structures exist, but they do not yet depend on the individual for survival.

How Capacity Failure Shows Up Here

When capacity fails at the individual contributor level, the signs are usually visible and localized:

i. Missed or inconsistent deadlines

ii. Fluctuating quality of output

iii. Burnout from poor boundaries or overwork

iv. Stagnation caused by unaddressed skill gaps

v. Disengagement or loss of motivation.

Importantly, failure at this level rarely causes systemic damage. The impact is contained. Correction is often possible through training, rest, or clearer expectations.

This containment is one of the reasons this level feels manageable, and why many people thrive here.

The Hidden Strength of This Level

Individual contributor capacity rewards focus. It allows:

i. Deep mastery

ii. Precision

iii. Efficiency

iv. And personal ownership of outcomes.

Many people are strongest at this level, and there is no shame in that. In fact, organizations collapse when they undervalue individual contributors or pressure everyone toward leadership roles they were never designed for.

Excellence here is real excellence.

The danger does not lie in remaining an individual contributor. It lies in misunderstanding what excellence here prepares you for— and what it does not.

Where the Misalignment Begins

The most common misalignment occurs when excellence at this level is mistaken for readiness for the next.

High-performing individual contributors often assume leadership is simply an extension of what they already do:

i. More responsibility

ii. More tasks

iii. Higher standards

iv. Greater visibility.

They believe that if they keep improving their competence, leadership will naturally follow.

It will not.

The First Misalignment:
When Doing Is Confused with Leading

Leadership does not add tasks. It changes the nature of responsibility.

At the individual contributor level:

i. Effort directly produces results

ii. Success is personally earned

iii. And accountability is largely self-contained.

At leadership levels:

i. Effort does not scale outcomes

ii. Results depend on others

iii. And accountability expands beyond personal control.

This distinction is critical.

Many of the most technically skilled professionals struggle as leaders not because they lack intelligence or commitment, but because they were never required to rebuild capacity for people, only for performance.

They excelled at doing. They were not trained for bearing.

Why Skill Stops Being the Differentiator

At the individual contributor level, skill differentiates. At higher levels, skill is assumed.

Leadership roles do not ask: Can you execute?

They ask:

Can you absorb complexity?

Can you regulate emotion under pressure?

Can you lead people who think, feel, and perform differently than you?

Can you remain functional when outcomes are no longer directly tied to your effort?

These are not skill questions. They are capacity questions.

A Critical Truth about This Level

Individual contributor capacity is necessary but insufficient for leadership. It is a foundation, not a ceiling.

When leaders fail to recognize this, they attempt to solve leadership challenges with execution tools. They work harder, take on more, and centralize responsibility. For a while, it appears effective.

Then strain appears. Then fatigue. Then breakdown.

Not because they were unqualified, but because the capacity required had changed.

Why This Level Still Matters

No leader outgrows the need for individual contributor capacity. Even at higher levels:

i.   Personal discipline matters

ii. boundary awareness matters

iii. Stamina matters

iv. And clarity of execution matters.

What changes is that these are no longer sufficient on their own. They must be integrated into broader relational and structural capacity.

That integration begins at the next level.

Understanding individual contributor capacity clarifies an essential leadership reality: excellence at one level does not automatically prepare you for the next.

Capacity must evolve as responsibility expands.

The next level introduces a decisive shift—away from personal execution and toward relational accountability. It is here that many leaders encounter their first real ceiling.

We turn to that transition next.

Level Two: Team Leader Capacity

The transition from individual contributor to team leader is one of the most underestimated shifts in leadership development. It is often treated as a promotion in responsibility, when it is a reconstruction of capacity.

This is the level where leadership stops being primarily about doing and becomes fundamentally about people.

Many leaders assume they are prepared for this transition because they are competent, trained, and credentialed. They are not.

I learned this personally.

Despite a structured pathway into leadership, including six months of streamlined training for the role, another six months of formal orientation, multiple week-long leadership retreats, and an assigned coach, the transition exposed limits I did not know existed. What followed was not a smooth ascent, but a prolonged adjustment that took years rather than months.

It took over five years to fully build the capacity required to move from managing people to leading them.

That distinction matters.

What Changes at the Team Leader Level

At the team leader level, responsibility shifts from personal execution to collective performance.

You are no longer primarily accountable for what you produce. You are accountable for:

i.   How others perform,

ii. How they are developed

iii. How conflict is handled

iv. How trust is built or eroded

v. And how outcomes are achieved through people rather than effort.

This level introduces a new category of weight: relational weight.

Unlike task-based pressure, relational weight is unpredictable. It cannot be scheduled, optimized, or fully controlled. It includes:

i. Personality differences

ii. Emotional reactions

iii. Unspoken expectations

iv. Unresolved tension

v. And competing motivations.

Technical excellence does not prepare leaders for this weight.

Why Training Alone Is Insufficient

Formal training teaches skills. Capacity is built through exposure, repetition, failure, and recalibration.

Leadership development programs often assume that proximity to information produces transformation. It does not. *Knowing how to lead and being built to lead are not the same.*

At the team leader level, leaders discover:

i. that people do not respond like systems,

ii. that logic does not dissolve emotion,

iii. that consistency does not eliminate resistance,

iv. and that authority does not equal influence.

These realizations are not intellectual. They are experiential. And they are destabilizing without sufficient capacity.

Managing People vs. Leading People

Managing people focuses on:

i. Compliance

ii. Output

iii. Schedules

iv. And performance metrics.

Leading people requires:

i. Discernment,

ii. Emotional regulation

iii. Patience

iv. Adaptability

v. And trust-building.

Managing relies on structure. Leading relies on capacity.

At this level, leaders must learn to:

i. Absorb dissatisfaction without retaliation

ii. Correct without humiliating

iii. Delegate without losing control

iv. And remain steady when others are not.

This is where many leaders regress.

How Capacity Failure Shows Up at This Level

When team leader capacity is insufficient, failure appears subtly, and becomes normalized: micromanagement replaces trust, high performers are overused while others disengage, conflict is avoided or mishandled, leaders become emotionally reactive, retention declines, the leader becomes indispensable, and exhausted.

Results may still be achieved, but they are person-dependent, not system-supported.

This is a warning sign.

When outcomes collapse in the leader's absence, capacity has not been built, it has been compensated for.

The False Comfort of Control

One of the most common traps at this level is control.

Leaders who excelled as individual contributors often default to control when outcomes feel threatened. They step in, take over, redo work, and centralize decisions. In the short term, this restores stability.

In the long term, it destroys capacity.

Control feels productive. It is limiting.

Capacity at the team leader level requires relinquishing the illusion that outcomes must pass through you to be valid.

The Emotional Work of Team Leadership

This level introduces emotional labor that cannot be delegated:

i.   Managing disappointment

ii.   Carrying unresolved tension

iii. Receiving criticism

iv.   And making decisions that cannot please everyone.

Without emotional capacity, leaders either:

i.   Discharge pressure onto others

ii.   Internalize it until burnout or

iii. Withdraw relationally.

None of these scale.

Capacity at this level requires learning how to hold emotional weight without distortion.

This is rarely taught. It must be built.

The Turning Point:
When Presence Becomes Optional

As capacity increases, something fundamental shifts.

Leadership becomes less dependent on physical presence. Outcomes stabilize without constant oversight. Trust replaces surveillance. Systems begin to carry what effort once sustained.

This was the point at which my own leadership expanded.

I moved from managing a single clinic to overseeing additional projects and programs alongside my primary responsibility. Eventually, that expanded to multiple clinics, not because I was doing more, but because my presence was no longer required for the system to function.

This is a defining marker of team leader capacity.

When leadership works only when you are present, capacity is limited.

When leadership continues in your absence, capacity has been built.

What Capacity Looks Like at This Level

Team leader capacity includes:

   i.   Emotional regulation under pressure

   ii. Relational discernment

   iii. Clarity in communication

   iv. Delegation without disengagement

   v.   Accountability without domination

   vi. And trust without naivety.

This is not about personality. It is about structure.

Leaders who build this capacity create teams that:

   i.   Function without heroics

   ii. Absorb change without collapse

   iii. And sustain performance over time.

Why This Level Takes Time

The team leader level is where many leaders either plateau or mature.

It takes time because:

i.   People are not predictable

ii. Relational patterns must be unlearned

iii. Trust must be earned **repeatedly**

iv. And leadership identity must shift.

There is no shortcut here.

Capacity is built through:

i.   Repetition

ii. Feedback

iii. Failure

iv. Reflection

v.   Recalibration.

The Hidden Reward of This Level

The reward of team leader capacity is scale without exhaustion.

When built correctly:

i.   Leadership becomes sustainable

ii. Growth no longer requires constant intervention,

iii. Influence expands without personal depletion.

This is the first level where leaders glimpse what it means to lead through others rather than over them.

The team leader level exposes a critical truth: leadership is not validated by how much you can manage, but by how much can function without you.

Level Three: Organizational Leader Capacity

The transition from team leadership to organizational leadership introduces a profound, and often unsettling shift. Responsibility moves beyond relationships and into systems, compliance, and collective consequence. At this level, leadership is no longer primarily relational. It becomes structural, ethical, and strategic.

This is the level where leadership begins to test values, not rhetorically, but operationally.

Organizational leaders are required to make decisions that are:

i. Correct but unpopular

ii. Necessary but emotionally costly

iii. Legally sound but relationally disruptive.

Capacity at this level is not measured by likability or accessibility. It is measured by stewardship under pressure.

What Changes at the Organizational Level

At the organizational level, accountability expands dramatically.

Leaders are now responsible for:

i.   Regulatory compliance at state and federal levels,

ii. Financial viability and risk exposure

iii. Institutional reputation

iv. Long-term sustainability

v.   And outcomes that affect people they may not know personally.

Decisions are no longer judged solely by intent or effort. They are judged by impact, precedent, and consequence.

This level introduces a different kind of weight: systemic weight.

Here, leadership requires the ability to:

i.   Separate personal sentiment from organizational responsibility

ii. Make unemotional decisions in emotionally charged environments

iii. And hold clarity when others experience confusion or fear.

When People Become Statistics—and Why That Matters

One of the most difficult realities of organizational leadership is that individual stories must sometimes yield to systemic necessity.

This does not mean people stop mattering. It means decisions are evaluated through a different lens.

I remember an incident that crystallized this reality for me.

A staff member, someone with whom I had a cordial and friendly relationship, had to be terminated. The decision had nothing to do with personal dislike. It was rooted in regulatory, operational, and organizational considerations that could not be ignored without jeopardizing the business.

Before the termination occurred, we had already scheduled a staff dinner to celebrate a milestone. It was neither practical nor appropriate to exclude her. That Saturday evening, she sat beside me. The conversation was casual. The atmosphere was warm. Nothing outwardly signaled what was coming.

On the following Monday, I handed her the termination letter.

The difficulty was not only the decision itself, but the aftershock.

It was not her reaction that lingered. It was the way others processed it.

Months later, after another organizational win, I invited my core team out for dinner. Shortly afterward, one team member reached out privately and said, "I hope this isn't another last supper."

At first, I did not understand what she meant, so I asked for clarity. She explained that after witnessing how the previous termination unfolded—how the staff dinner had appeared warm and ordinary, and how the termination followed the next business day without any outward emotional cues—she had become afraid of me. Her words were honest and painful: "I don't really trust you anymore."

That moment stayed with me.

Not because the decision had been wrong, it was necessary and defensible, but because it revealed a critical reality of organizational leadership: decisions are not only evaluated by their correctness, but by how they are interpreted by those who are not privy to the full context.

At this level, leaders carry consequences far beyond the individual decision. They carry the emotional reactions, the assumptions, and the narratives that form around their actions— often without the ability to correct every misinterpretation without compromising governance or confidentiality.

It hurt. But it also clarified something essential.

Organizational leadership is not designed to preserve comfort or emotional reassurance. It is designed to protect the mission, the system, and the people collectively—even when that protection is misunderstood.

This is part of the cost of capacity at this level.

Why This Is a Capacity Issue—Not a Character Flaw

Organizational leadership forces leaders to operate in tension:

i.   Between warmth and firmness

ii. Between accessibility and authority

iii. Between empathy and enforcement.

Leaders who lack capacity at this level often respond in one of two unhealthy ways: They avoid necessary decisions to preserve relationships. They become emotionally detached to protect themselves.

Both approaches damage the organization.

Capacity at this level is the ability to:

i.   Act without cruelty

ii. Decide without resentment

iii. And remain human without becoming hostage to emotion.

This is not coldness. It is governance.

Why Personal Values Are Tested Here

This level of leadership demands constant reassessment of personal values and guiding principles.

Questions emerge that cannot be answered theoretically:

What do I prioritize when compliance and compassion collide?

How do I honor people while protecting the institution?

Where do I draw the line between empathy and responsibility?

Organizational leaders must develop ethical capacity—the ability to make decisions that are:

i.   Defensible

ii. Repeatable

iii. And aligned with long-term integrity.

Good intentions are insufficient. Consistency matters more than sentiment.

The Illusion of Friendship at This Level

One of the hardest lessons at this level is understanding that perceived closeness does not change responsibility.

Leaders may appear friendly. They may care deeply about their teams. But organizational leadership cannot be governed by personal preference.

This is often misunderstood by teams.

What some interpret as betrayal is boundary clarity.

At this level:

i.   Friendliness is not a contract

ii. Access is not immunity

iii. And proximity does not override policy.

Leaders who fail to establish this clarity either become manipulable, or paralyzed.

Capacity Failure at the Organizational Level

When capacity is insufficient here, failure manifests as:

i.   Inconsistent enforcement of standards

ii. Ethical drift under pressure

iii. Avoidance of difficult decisions

iv. Reactive leadership

v.   Reputational damage.

Sometimes leaders attempt to soften hard decisions through over-explanation or appeasement. This rarely works. It erodes confidence and creates uncertainty.

Capacity at this level requires calm authority.

What Capacity Looks Like at This Level

Organizational leader capacity includes:

i.   Systems thinking

ii. Regulatory awareness

iii. Ethical consistency

iv. Emotional restraint

v. Decisiveness without hostility

vi. The ability to hold long-term perspective.

It also includes the ability to absorb misunderstanding.

Not everyone will understand your decisions. Not everyone should.

Leadership at this level is not about being liked. It is about being trusted to steward the organization.

Why This Level Is Lonely

Organizational leadership introduces a form of loneliness that cannot be resolved through connection alone.

Some information cannot be shared. Some decisions cannot be discussed. Some burdens cannot be distributed.

Capacity here includes the ability to carry solitude without distortion.

Leaders who lack this capacity often:

i. Over-disclose

ii. Seek validation from subordinates

iii. Retreat emotionally

None of these preserve trust.

The Reward of Organizational Capacity

When capacity is built at this level:

i. Organizations stabilize

ii. Systems function without constant crisis

iii. Compliance becomes culture rather than enforcement

iv. Leaders gain the freedom to think strategically rather than reactively.

This is the level where leadership begins to outlive personality.

Organizational leadership introduces a sobering realization: responsibility increases faster than understanding, and impact extends farther than visibility.

Beyond this level lies an even greater challenge, system stewardship, where decisions shape institutions, cultures, and outcomes long after leaders are gone.

At that level, capacity is no longer personal. It is historical.

Level Four: System Steward Capacity

System steward capacity represents the highest and most consequential level of responsibility. It is leadership that no longer centers on proximity, presence, or personality. At this level, influence is embedded, not performed. Outcomes are carried by systems, not individuals.

System stewards do not manage people directly. They shape the environments, structures, values, and frameworks that govern how people live, lead, and decide—often without ever meeting them.

This is the level where leadership becomes generational.

What Distinguishes System Stewardship

At this level, leadership responsibility shifts again, this time away from organizations and toward ecosystems.

System stewards are accountable for: frameworks that outlive their tenure, cultures that reproduce themselves, ideas that travel independently, and systems that function without direct supervision.

They do not ask, "How do I lead this group?"

They ask, "What must exist, so leadership continues without me?"

This is not a question of charisma or visibility. It is a question of design.

Why Presence Becomes Irrelevant at This Level

Earlier levels of leadership still depend, at least partially, on the leader's physical or relational presence. System stewardship does not.

At this level:

i.   Presence is replaced by process

ii. Instruction is replaced by formation

iii. And personality is replaced by principle.

The measure of success is no longer whether people follow you, but whether they continue in alignment without you.

This is the truest test of capacity.

A Living Example of System Steward Capacity

One of the clearest examples of this level of leadership is Dr. Myles Munroe.

I choose to reference him deliberately, not only because of his global influence, but because I was alive during his lifetime and have watched his impact persist beyond it.

If you have ever traveled to the Bahamas and visited the Diplomat Centre, the institutional equivalent of his church, you will immediately recognize something significant: his legacy was never anchored in a building.

It was anchored in people.

Dr. Munroe did not attempt to disciple everyone personally. He did not rely on proximity. He did not centralize influence.

Instead, he built a system of transformation.

Through structured teaching, codified principles, leadership development pipelines, and reproducible frameworks, he influenced millions, most of whom he never met one-on-one.

That is system stewardship.

Why This Example Matters

This example matters because it corrects a common misunderstanding about legacy.

Legacy is not visibility. Legacy is not size. Legacy is not longevity of a name.

Legacy is continuity of impact.

Dr. Munroe's influence did not diminish when his physical presence ended because:

i.   The ideas were codified

ii. The systems were functional

iii. The leaders were developed

iv. The values were transferable.

The architect passed. The structure remained. The system continued to produce.

This is the hallmark of system steward capacity.

System Stewardship Is Not About Control

One of the most dangerous misconceptions about system-level leadership is that it requires tighter control. System stewards must relinquish control earlier than anyone else.

Why?

Because systems cannot scale if they depend on approval, proximity, or constant correction.

System stewardship requires:

i.   Trust in structure

ii. Clarity of values

iii. Confidence in reproduction.

Control produces compliance. Systems produce continuity.

Why Many Leaders Never Reach This Level

Most leaders do not fail to reach this level because they lack intelligence or effort. They fail because they are unwilling to:

   i. Decentralize authority

  ii. Release ownership

 iii. Allow others to carry influence without personal validation.

System stewardship requires ego maturity.

The leader must be willing to:

   i. Be referenced rather than consulted

  ii. Be honored rather than obeyed

 iii. Be followed in absence.

This level exposes insecurity faster than any other.

The Ethical Weight of System Stewardship

System stewards carry an ethical burden that exceeds all previous levels.

Why?

Because systems amplify values.

If ethics are flawed at this level, the damage is not temporary, it is durable. Harm becomes embedded. Injustice becomes normalized. Dysfunction becomes inherited.

History demonstrates this repeatedly:

   i. Systems outlive intentions

  ii. Structures outlast architects

 iii. And consequences persist across generations.

This is why ethical capacity is non-negotiable at this level.

System stewards must design with foresight, humility, and restraint.

Why You May Not Be "Here Yet"— and Why That's Fine

Most leaders will never operate fully at this level. And that is not failure.

System stewardship is not a reward. It is a responsibility.

Some leaders are called to build organizations. Others to steward institutions. Others to shape nations, industries, or movements.

What matters is alignment, not ambition.

Understanding this level early allows leaders to prepare responsibly rather than arrive prematurely.

The Highest Form of Capacity

At the system steward level, capacity is measured by one question: What continues to function, produce, and align long after I am gone?

When leadership reaches this level:

i. Succession is natural

ii. Continuity is intentional

iii. Legacy is inevitable.

This is leadership that survives its leader.

Understanding system stewardship reframes the entire conversation about leadership.

Capacity failure is rarely dramatic.

It is normalized—until collapse.

Most leadership failures do not begin with scandal, incompetence, or rebellion. They begin quietly, with small accommodations and unexamined strain.

What eventually looks like sudden breakdown is almost always the result of long-standing architectural mismatch that was tolerated for too long.

Capacity failure does not announce itself as failure. It presents as pressure.

Leaders experience:

i.   Longer hours

ii. Constant urgency

iii. Persistent fatigue

iv. Increased emotional reactivity

v.   Diminishing margin.

Because results may still be achieved, at least temporarily, these warning signs are often interpreted as dedication rather than danger. Leaders compensate with effort. They work harder. They push through. They normalize overload.

But effort is not capacity. It is a temporary substitute for structure.

Why Failure Looks Sudden—but Is Not

Collapse only appears sudden to observers who were not watching the architecture.

Those paying attention to structure can often see it coming:

i. Responsibility expanding without redesign

ii. Decisions centralizing instead of distributing

iii. Emotional strain accumulating without processing

iv. Systems relying increasingly on heroics

v. Leaders becoming indispensable instead of scalable.

These are not signs of commitment. They are indicators of capacity strain.

When leaders attempt to carry new levels of responsibility using old internal frameworks, failure is not a possibility, it is a matter of timing.

The Predictable Pattern of Capacity Failure

Across levels, capacity failure tends to follow a predictable sequence: First, strain appears. Then compensation begins. Then overload becomes normalized. Then cracks are explained away. Then collapse occurs.

At the individual contributor level, this may look like burnout or stagnation. At the team leader level, it appears as micromanagement, attrition, or relational breakdown. At the organizational level, it manifests as ethical drift, inconsistent enforcement, or reputational damage. At the system level, it produces generational dysfunction that outlives the leader.

The scale changes. The pattern does not.

Why Leaders Miss the Warning Signs

Leaders often miss capacity failure because they are measuring the wrong indicators.

They assess:

i. Output instead of sustainability

ii. Growth instead of governance

iii. Opportunity instead of readiness

iv. Visibility instead of structure.

As long as results continue, capacity gaps remain hidden. But results are lagging indicators. Architecture is the leading one.

This is why some leaders fail upward advancing into roles that expose weaknesses rather than resolving them.

Capacity Failure Is Not a Moral Judgment

It is critical to state this clearly: Capacity failure is not a character flaw. It is not a lack of intelligence. It is not a deficit of passion or calling.

It is structural.

Leaders are rarely undone by what they cannot do. They are undone by what they are required to carry without having been rebuilt for it.

Until leaders understand how capacity fails, they will continue to: confuse promotion with preparation, mistake access for readiness, interpret exhaustion as sacrifice, and spiritualize breakdown instead of redesigning structure.

Capacity failure is not a surprise. It is a warning ignored.

The Critical Shift

Before responsibility expands, capacity must be rebuilt.

Not after pressure exposes the gap. Not after damage has occurred. Not after trust has been eroded.

Before.

This requires leaders to stop asking, "What more can I do?" and begin asking, "What must be strengthened to carry what is coming?"

That question changes everything.

Now that we have examined how capacity failure shows up, the next step is practical and unavoidable.

Understanding failure patterns is not enough.

Leaders must learn how to build capacity deliberately, before pressure demands it, before opportunity exposes it, and before responsibility outpaces readiness.

That is where we turn next.

Without a workflow, leaders rely on personality, stamina, and crisis management. That may work temporarily, but it is not scalable. Workflow replaces heroics with structure.

Dr. Joke Solanke

CHAPTER 9

◆———————————————◆

Building Capacity Deliberately
(The Workflow)

———

C apacity is designed—not hoped for.

Most people do not fail because they lack desire. They fail because they lack design.

Desire is abundant. Vision is common. Ambition is everywhere. What is rare is intentional architecture, the disciplined work of preparing structure before pressure arrives.

When leaders talk about capacity, it is often treated as something mystical or intuitive—something you either have or don't have. It is described as gifting, temperament, calling, or luck. But capacity is none of these things.

Capacity is architecture. And architecture does not happen accidentally. Architecture is designed, reviewed, tested, reinforced, and only then implemented. Anything else is improvisation—and improvisation underweight is collapse waiting for a moment.

This is why a workflow is not optional. It is protective.

Without a workflow, "capacity building" becomes a motivational slogan rather than a functional discipline. People respond with intensity instead of intention. They work harder instead of redesigning. They accelerate activity instead of strengthening structure.

They increase effort, while quietly weakening the very systems meant to sustain them.

Capacity is not built by force. It is built by sequence.

The Architecture Metaphor: Why Preparation Precedes Use

No serious architect starts with construction. Before a single brick is laid, there is a long and largely invisible process that most people never see—and rarely celebrate.

There are:

i. Site assessments

ii. Soil testing

iii. Environmental considerations

iv. Load calculations

v. Zoning restrictions

vi. Material analysis

vii. Stress modeling

viii. Safety contingencies.

This preparatory phase often takes longer than the visible building phase. It consumes time, expertise, and resources—yet produces nothing immediately tangible.

To the untrained eye, it looks like delay. To the trained eye, it is wisdom.

Skipping preparation does not save time. It simply borrows failure from the future. The higher the structure, the more essential the unseen work becomes. Capacity works the same way.

Why People Resist Preparation

Preparation feels inefficient to anyone who equates progress with movement. In a culture that rewards speed, visibility, and output, preparation can look like:

i.   hesitation

ii. Overthinking

iii. Lack of confidence

iv. Unnecessary caution.

But preparation is not fear. It is respect for weight, time, and consequence.

Most leaders underestimate what future responsibility will demand because they evaluate the next level emotionally instead of structurally. They imagine success without accounting for pressure. They desire influence without building endurance. They want scale without recalibrating stability.

So, they enter new levels with old structures. And strain begins immediately.

The Cost of Implementation without Preparation

Implementation without preparation is one of the most expensive leadership mistakes.

It produces:

i.   Burnout disguised as dedication

ii. Urgency mistaken for productivity

iii. Heroics compensating for weak systems

iv. Emotional volatility blamed on stress

v.   Repeated crises labeled "the nature of leadership."

These are not normal. They are signals.

When systems require constant intervention to survive, capacity was not built, it was assumed. When leaders become indispensable to daily function, structure has failed. When success cannot be repeated without exhaustion, the vessel is too small.

These are not motivational problems. They are architectural ones.

Why Capacity Requires a Workflow

A workflow does three essential things:

It slows the process enough to make growth safe. Capacity grows under measured exposure—not reckless expansion.

It introduces sequence instead of urgency. Certain things must be strengthened before other things can be added.

It makes capacity intentional rather than accidental. What is designed can be sustained. What is improvised must be maintained by effort.

> *Without a workflow, leaders rely on personality, stamina, and crisis management. That may work temporarily, but it is not scalable. Workflow replaces heroics with structure.*

Preparation Is an Investment, Not a Delay

Some of the least visible seasons are the most consequential.

Preparation rarely feels rewarding. It requires restraint, introspection, planning, and the humility to admit that something is not yet ready.

But preparation is where collapse is prevented.

In architecture, the costliest failures are not cosmetic—they are foundational. And by the time foundational failure becomes visible, repair is no longer simple. It is invasive, expensive, and sometimes impossible without demolition.

Capacity failures work the same way. By the time burnout, ethical compromise, relational breakdown, or systemic failure becomes visible, the opportunity for easy correction has passed.

That is why capacity must be built before expansion—not after damage occurs.

Capacity Is Contextual, So the Workflow Must Be Flexible

This workflow applies whether you are: an individual seeking personal stability, a team leader scaling through people, an organizational leader managing systems and compliance, or a system steward shaping frameworks that outlive you.

The principles stay consistent. The application is contextual. Architecture adjusts to terrain. Capacity adjusts to responsibility.

The workflow is not rigid, but it insists on the same sequence of thinking.

Why Sequence Matters More Than Speed

Many leaders are willing to work hard. Few are willing to work in order.

Sequence forces patience. Sequence exposes gaps. Sequence demands humility.

It makes leaders ask:

i.   What must be stabilized before we expand?

ii. What strain am I normalizing?

iii. What am I compensating for with effort?

iv. What would collapse if I stepped away?

These questions are uncomfortable, but protective.

Capacity does not reward speed. It rewards order.

This is not a productivity system. It is not a performance framework. It is not a checklist for faster growth.

It is a design process for sustainability.

The goal is not to do more. The goal is to carry more without breaking.

In the sections that follow, we will walk through the workflow step by step, slowly, deliberately, and honestly, so that what you build can hold what is coming.

Because overflow is never the problem. The vessel is.

Step One: Honest Assessment

Why Capacity Building Always Begins With Truth

Capacity cannot be built on assumption. It must be built on truth.

Honest assessment is the most avoided, and most essential, step in capacity building. Not because it is complex, but because it is confronting. It forces leaders to pause momentum long enough to examine reality. And momentum is often mistaken for progress.

Many leaders move quickly because slowing down feels dangerous. They fear that assessment will expose weakness, stall advancement, or invite judgment. Assessment does the opposite. It protects leaders from being promoted into fragility.

Capacity does not collapse because leaders are unaware of their strengths. It collapses because they are unaware of their strain.

Honest assessment is not self-criticism. It is structural clarity.

The Difference between Self-Awareness and Honest Assessment

Self-awareness is knowing how you feel about your leadership. Honest assessment is understanding how your leadership functions.

Many leaders confuse reflection with evaluation.

Reflection is internal. Assessment is architectural.

Reflection asks, How do I experience this role?

Assessment asks, What is this role demanding—and what is currently carrying that demand?

A leader can feel confident and still be structurally overextended. A system can appear successful and still be internally unstable.

Assessment does not ask whether things are working. It asks what is holding them together.

Why Leaders Avoid This Step

Leaders avoid honest assessment for predictable reasons:

Past success distorts perception. What worked before is assumed to be sufficient now.

Busyness masks strain. Constant activity feels productive, even when it is compensatory.

Responsibility discourages vulnerability. Leaders fear that naming limits will undermine confidence.

Comparison replaces clarity. Leaders measure themselves against others rather than against the weight they carry.

But capacity does not respond to comparison. It responds to load.

What Honest Assessment Is—and Is Not

Honest assessment is not:

i.   A performance review

ii. A personality test

iii. A moral evaluation

iv. A justification exercise.

It is a load-bearing analysis.

It examines:

i.   What is being carried

ii. How it is being carried

iii. Where strain is accumulating

iv. What would fail if pressure increased.

Honest assessment does not ask, "Can I handle this?"

It asks, "What happens if this continues?"

The Core Question of Honest Assessment

Every honest assessment begins with one central question: What am I currently carrying that exceeds what was designed for this season?

This question reframes leadership evaluation away from ambition and toward sustainability.

It forces leaders to examine:

i. Responsibilities that quietly expanded

ii. Decisions that became emotionally heavier

iii. Systems that require constant intervention

iv. Relationships that consume disproportionate energy,

v. Roles that evolved without structural adjustment.

Capacity failure rarely begins with collapse. It begins with silent overload.

Domains That Must Be Assessed

Honest assessment must be multidimensional. Leaders often assess one area, usually performance, while ignoring others that are quietly deteriorating.

At minimum, assessment must examine five domains:

1. **Personal Load**

This domain evaluates how leadership demand is affecting the leader's physical and emotional reserves over time.

i. Energy levels across sustained periods

ii. Speed of physical and emotional recovery

iii. Boundary violations normalized as commitment

iv. Rest patterns that are reactive rather than intentional

The central question here is not, *Can I push through?* It is, *what is the cost of pushing through repeatedly?*

2. **Mental and Emotional Load**

This domain reveals how pressure is being processed internally

i.   Decision fatigue

ii. Emotional reactivity under pressure

iii. Rumination or avoidance

iv. Internal narratives shaped by past failures or trauma

This domain reveals whether the leader is regulating pressure or being regulated by it.

3. **Relational Load**

This domain assesses the health and distribution of relational responsibility.

i.   Concentration of conflict

ii. Erosion of trust

iii. Over-dependence on a few people

iv. Difficulty collaborating with different personalities

Relational strain is often misattributed to "people problems" when it is capacity misalignment.

4. **Structural Load**

This domain examines whether systems can carry responsibility independent of the leader

i.   Systems dependent on personal presence

ii. Processes that break under volume

iii. Roles that are unclear or overlapping

iv. Governance gaps masked by competence

Structure reveals whether leadership is scalable—or merely survivable.

5. **Ethical Load**

This domain evaluates how sustained pressure affects moral clarity and judgment.

i. Decisions that require moral compromise

ii. Rationalizations that repeat

iii. Pressure to sacrifice values for speed or approval

iv. Fatigue that blurs judgment

Ethical erosion rarely starts with intention. It starts with exhaustion.

The Most Important Insight of This Step

Honest assessment does not disqualify leaders. It protects them.

Capacity gaps are not evidence of inadequacy. They are evidence of transition.

Every new level introduces weight that old structures were never meant to carry. Assessment simply names that reality before damage occurs.

Unacknowledged gaps are dangerous.

Acknowledged gaps are buildable.

The Courage to Name Limits

One of the most mature acts of leadership is the willingness to name limits without shame.

Limitations are not deficiencies. They are design indicators.

A leader who refuses to acknowledge limits compensates with effort. A leader who names limits redesigns structure.

This is why honest assessment must be done before capacity building begins. Otherwise, leaders attempt to build on misdiagnosed problems, strengthening the wrong areas while ignoring the real points of strain.

What Honest Assessment Produces

When done well, honest assessment produces:

i. Clarity instead of confusion

ii. Focus instead of scattered effort

iii. Restraint instead of overextension

iv. Direction instead of anxiety.

It does not immediately relieve pressure. It explains it.

And explanation is the first form of relief.

A Diagnostic Pause

Before moving to the next step, ask yourself, without defensiveness or exaggeration:

i. Where am I currently compensating with effort?

ii. What responsibilities have expanded without redesign?

iii. What breaks first when pressure increases?

iv. What would fail if I stepped away for thirty days?

v. What am I avoiding naming because it feels inconvenient?

These questions are not accusatory. They are architectural.

Why This Step Cannot Be Skipped

Every failed capacity-building effort skips this step.

People rush to habits, delegation, discipline, or strategy, without understanding what those interventions are meant to support. The result is improvement without alignment.

Honest assessment ensures that capacity building addresses the actual load, not the imagined one.

Only after reality is clearly seen can structure be responsibly redesigned.

Assessment names the truth. But naming alone does not change structure.

Capacity does not fail everywhere at once.

It fails where strain is ignored the longest.

Step Two: Identifying Strain Points

Capacity does not collapse globally. It fails selectively.

Most leaders imagine capacity failure as dramatic and sudden— burnout, scandal, resignation, collapse. In reality, failure begins quietly in specific places where weight accumulates without reinforcement. These places are strain points.

A strain point is not where effort is lowest. It is where pressure exceeds structure.

Until strain is identified, leaders misinterpret symptoms. They attempt to solve systemic issues with personal effort, relational issues with authority, and ethical tension with justification. None of these resolve strain. They conceal it.

Identifying strain points is the bridge between awareness and redesign.

What a Strain Point Is (and Is Not)

A strain point is not:

i.   A weakness

ii. A moral failure

iii. A lack of discipline

iv. A personality flaw.

A strain point is a load-bearing mismatch, where demand has increased but structure has not.

Strain reveals where:

i.   Responsibility expanded silently

ii. Complexity increased without support

iii. Expectations changed without clarification

iv. Pressure became prolonged rather than temporary.

Every leader has strain points. What differentiates sustainable leaders from collapsing ones is not the absence of strain, but the willingness to locate it early.

Why Leaders Miss Strain Points

Strain points are often invisible because leaders normalize them.

Common normalization patterns include:

"This is just a busy season."

"Everyone at this level feels this way."

"I'll fix it once things slow down."

"This is what leadership costs."

These explanations are comforting, and dangerous.

Strain that is normalized becomes structural weakness. Structural weakness eventually becomes failure.

The Core Question of Step Two

Step One asked: What am I carrying?

Step Two asks: Where is what I'm carrying already causing distortion?

Strain is detected not by asking how much you are doing, but by observing what is bending, breaking, or requiring constant compensation.

Primary Categories of Strain

Strain appears predictably across five categories. Leaders must examine each honestly.

1. **Time Strain**

Time strain occurs when:

   i.   Everything feels urgent

   ii. Decisions are constantly reactive

   iii. Planning is postponed by crises

   iv. Rest is optional rather than structural.

Time strain is not about hours worked. It is about lack of margin.

When time strain persists, leaders:

   i.   Lose strategic perspective

   ii. Rush decisions

   iii. And confuse motion with progress.

Time strain reveals that capacity has been outpaced by pace.

2. **Emotional Strain**

Emotional strain appears when

   i.   irritability increases,

   ii. Patience shortens

   iii. Feedback feels personal

   iv. Leaders oscillate between withdrawal and reactivity.

This is often misdiagnosed as stress intolerance. It is not. Emotional strain indicates that leaders are absorbing emotional weight without sufficient regulation or support.

Pressure is being internalized rather than processed. Unchecked emotional strain erodes judgment long before it affects performance.

3. **Relational Strain**

Relational strain becomes visible

i.   Trust decreases

ii. Communication becomes guarded

iii. Collaboration feels exhausting

iv. Conflict accumulates without resolution.

Leaders often blame people at this stage. But relational strain is rarely about who is involved. It is about how relationships are being carried.

Relational strain reveals capacity gaps in:

i.   Discernment

ii. Delegation

iii. Expectation setting

iv. Boundary clarity.

4. **Structural Strain**

Structural strain is present when:

i.   Systems require heroics to function

ii. Outcomes depend on one person

iii. Processes break under growth

iv. Leaders cannot step away without disruption.

This strain is the most dangerous because it often masquerades as competence. Leaders who "hold everything together" are often praised, until exhaustion exposes the fragility of the structure. Structural strain indicates that effort is compensating for design failure.

5. **Ethical Strain**

Ethical strain appears subtly:

i. Repeated rationalizations

ii. Pressure to bend standards

iii. Silence in moments requiring courage

iv. Fatigue that dulls moral clarity.

Ethical strain rarely begins with wrongdoing. It begins with exhaustion and compromise framed as necessity. When leaders are overextended, values become negotiable—not intentionally, but incrementally. This is why ethical failure often follows prolonged strain, not sudden temptation.

How Strain Points Interact

Strain points rarely exist in isolation.

Time strain intensifies emotional strain. Emotional strain amplifies relational strain. Relational strain exposes structural strain. Structural strain accelerates ethical strain.

This cascading effect explains why leaders often feel overwhelmed without being able to name why.

Identifying strain points interrupts the cascade.

The Warning Signs Leaders Ignore

Certain signals consistently indicate unaddressed strain:

i.   Chronic urgency replacing planning

ii. Leaders becoming decision bottlenecks

iii. Emotional volatility under scrutiny

iv. Systems that only work when watched

v.   Success that cannot be repeated

vi. Exhaustion mislabeled as dedication

These are not personality traits. They are architectural warnings.

Why Naming Strain Feels Risky

Leaders hesitate to name strain because they fear:

i.   Appearing incapable

ii. Slowing momentum

iii. Disappointing others

iv. Exposing limits.

But strain exists whether it is named or not. Naming it does not create weakness. It creates direction.

Unidentified strain forces leaders to guess. Identified strain allows leaders to design.

A Practical Exercise: Mapping Strain

Before moving forward, leaders should complete this exercise honestly:

Ask:

i.   Where do I feel the most tension when responsibility increases?

ii. What requires constant attention to avoid failure?

iii. What breaks first when pressure rises?

iv. What am I secretly hoping does not get bigger?

v.   What would I redesign if I were starting again today?

The answers reveal strain points.

Why This Step Precedes Strengthening

Many leaders attempt to strengthen everything at once. This guarantees exhaustion.

Capacity is not expanded by reinforcing all areas equally. It is expanded by reinforcing the right areas first.

Strain points determine priority.

Without this step:

i.   Leaders overbuild in comfortable areas

ii. Ignore failing structures

iii. And misallocate energy

With this step:

i.   Effort becomes targeted

ii. Resources are conserved

iii. Growth becomes stable.

The Discipline of Staying Here Long Enough

Leaders often rush past strain identification because it feels uncomfortable and unproductive. But skipping this step ensures that later interventions fail.

This is the diagnostic phase. Nothing is built yet. But everything is clarified.

Design always follows diagnosis.

Step one revealed what you are carrying. Step two exposes where it is already causing strain.

The next step addresses the most counterintuitive discipline in capacity building: strengthening before expanding.

Because the instinct to grow is strong, but growth applied to weak structure does not produce progress.

It produces collapse.

We turn next to Step Three: *Strengthening Before Expanding*—where restraint becomes the most strategic act of leadership.

Step Three: Strengthening Before Expanding

Every instinct in leadership pushes toward expansion.

When opportunities appear, the reflex is to say yes. When demand increases, the impulse is to scale. When momentum builds, restraint feels like resistance.

But architecture teaches a different law:

Nothing should rise until what already exists can bear more weight.

Expansion is visible. Strengthening is invisible.

And because strengthening does not feel productive, leaders often skip it, only to discover later that what they built cannot hold.

Architecture Does Not Begin With Height

In construction, no architect starts by designing the upper floors.

They begin with:

i.   Soil analysis

ii. Load calculations

iii. Stress distribution

iv. Material limits

v.   Failure scenarios.

Most of this work happens before anything visible rises.

Leadership capacity follows the same logic.

If leaders expand responsibility before strengthening structure, they do not accelerate success, they accelerate exposure.

What "Strengthening" Actually Means

Strengthening is not doing more.

It is reinforcing what already exists so it can carry more without distortion.

In leadership terms, strengthening involves:

i. Deepening internal regulation,

ii. Reinforcing boundaries,

iii. Stabilizing systems,

v. Clarifying roles

vi. Reducing dependency on personal effort.

Strengthening prepares for growth without announcing it.

That is why it requires discipline.

The Illusion of Readiness

Leaders often confuse functioning with preparedness.

Just because something is working does not mean it is strong.

A structure can stand under current weight and still fail under increased load.

Many leadership failures occur not because leaders were incapable, but because they assumed current success meant future readiness.

Function answers: Is this working now?

Strength answers: Will this still work when pressure increases?

Load-Bearing vs Decorative Structures

In architecture, not every component carries weight.

Some elements are decorative. Others are load bearing.

Capacity failure occurs when leaders mistake decorative strengths for structural ones.

Examples:

i. Charisma mistaken for leadership depth

ii. Intelligence mistaken for decision stamina

iii. Activity mistaken for system health

iv. Visibility mistaken for authority

These elements enhance appearance, but they do not carry weight.

Strengthening focuses exclusively on load-bearing structures.

Where Leaders Must Strengthen First

After identifying strain points, leaders must reinforce the areas already absorbing the most pressure.

This typically includes:

i. Internal Structure

ii. Emotional regulation under prolonged pressure

iii. Decision clarity without urgency

iv. Stamina for unresolved tension

If the leader is the weakest structure, everything else will fail.

Relational Load Distribution

i. Delegation that removes dependency, not responsibility

ii. Clear expectations to reduce emotional friction

iii. Trust frameworks rather than personality reliance

Relationships must carry weight—not transfer it all upward.

System Integrity

i.   Processes that function without constant intervention

ii. Clear escalation paths

iii. Decision frameworks that reduce ambiguity

Systems exist to preserve leadership capacity—not replace it.

Ethical Reinforcement

i.   Reclarifying non-negotiables

ii. Removing gray zones created by exhaustion

iii. Ensuring consistency under pressure

Ethics weaken first when capacity is overstretched.

Why Leaders Resist This Step

Strengthening feels like slowing down.

It often requires:

i.   Saying no to good opportunities,

ii. Pausing growth initiatives,

iii. Redesigning roles,

iv. Confronting uncomfortable limitations.

Leaders fear that restraint will be misinterpreted as weakness.

But architecture proves the opposite:

Only weak structures rush upward without reinforcement.

Strong structures can wait.

The Cost of Skipping Strengthening

When strengthening is skipped:

i. Leaders compensate with effort

ii. Urgency replaces strategy

iii. Systems depend on heroics.

This works—temporarily.

But effort is finite. Structure is not.

Eventually, leaders become the load-bearing element for everything:

i. Decisions

ii. Conflicts

iii. Performance

iv. Stability.

That is not leadership. That is collapse postponed.

Strengthening Is Contextual, Not Global

Leaders often try to "fix everything" at once.

That is unnecessary, and exhausting.

Strengthening is targeted.

It focuses only on:

i. The most stressed structures,

ii. The most vulnerable systems,

iii. The areas where expansion would cause immediate rupture.

This precision conserves energy and increases effectiveness.

A Diagnostic Question for This Step

Before expanding anything, leaders must ask:

If what I am carrying increased by 30% tomorrow, what would fail first?

The answer reveals what must be strengthened now.

Why Strengthening Requires Time

Materials cure before they carry weight.

Concrete must set. Steel must settle. Foundations must stabilize.

Rushing this phase weakens everything built on it.

Similarly, leaders must allow time for:

i. Habits to embed,

ii. Systems to normalize,

iii. Teams to adapt, and trust to mature.

Time is not wasted here. It is invested.

The Quiet Confidence of Strengthened Leaders

Leaders who strengthen before expanding develop a distinct posture.

They are less reactive.
They move with restraint.
They do not rush visibility.
They are not intimidated by delay.

They know what their structure can carry.
That knowledge produces calm.

Strengthening prepares for growth without announcing it.
That is why it requires discipline.

Strengthening Is an Act of Stewardship

This step reframes leadership ambition.

The question is no longer, *How far can I go?*
It becomes, *What must I build so going further does not destroy what already exists?*

That is stewardship.
Not fear.
Not hesitation.
Wisdom.

Step One revealed what you are carrying.
Step Two exposed where strain exists.
Step Three stabilized the structure before growth resumes.

Only now does expansion become responsible.

The next step addresses what most leaders try to do too early: building relational and structural support so capacity is shared rather than centralized.

Step Four: Building Support before Scaling

Why Capacity Cannot Remain Centralized

One of the clearest signs that capacity has not yet been built is this: everything still depends on one person.

Decisions bottleneck at the top. Problems wait for one voice. Momentum pauses when one individual is absent.

This is not strength. It is exposure.

Architecture teaches a simple truth:

Any structure that relies on a single load-bearing column is fragile.

Leadership capacity must be distributed before it is expanded.

The Difference between Help and Support

Many leaders believe they already have support because people are around them.

But proximity is not support. Assistance is not architecture.

There is a difference between:
people who help occasionally,
and
systems that carry weight consistently.

Support, in the context of capacity, is not about kindness or availability. It is about load redistribution.

Why Leaders Resist This Step

Leaders often delay building support because:

Delegation feels risky, trust has been violated before, standards feel difficult to reproduce, or speed feels more efficient than collaboration.

In the short term, centralized leadership feels productive. In the long term, it guarantees exhaustion.

What leaders call "control" is often fear of failure. What they call "high standards" is often lack of systems.

Support Is Not About Releasing Responsibility

One of the most common misunderstandings about support is the belief that it weakens authority.

It does not.

Support does not remove accountability. It redistributes execution so accountability remains intact without overload.

Strong leaders do not abdicate responsibility. They design pathways for responsibility to travel without distortion.

Two Types of Support That Must Be Built

Capacity is preserved through two forms of support: relational support and structural support.

They serve different purposes. Both are necessary.

Relational Support: Who helps carry the weight?

Relational support answers the question: Who can absorb complexity with me?

This is not about loyalty. It is about complementarity.

Relational capacity is built when leaders:

Stop looking for replicas, stop demanding sameness, and start valuing difference.

Why Duplication Is Not the Goal

Many leaders unconsciously seek people who:

Think like them, work like them, communicate like them, and validate their approach.

This feels efficient. It is not resilient.

Duplication limits diversity. Diversity increases capacity.

Leadership does not scale through cloning. It scales through complementarity.

Relational support allows leaders to work with people who:

Process information differently, bring alternate strengths, challenge assumptions, and see blind spots the leader cannot.

The goal is not comfort. The goal is coverage.

Trust Is Not Automatic—It Is Designed

Leaders often say, "I don't trust easily." That may be true. But trust is not primarily emotional. It is structural.

Trust grows when:

Roles are clear, authority is defined, accountability is consistent, and consequences are predictable.

When trust depends on personality, it collapses under pressure. When trust is embedded in structure, it endures.

Structural Support: What Carries the Weight

Structural support answers a different question: What continues to function when I am unavailable?

This includes:

Decision frameworks, escalation paths, documented processes, role clarity, and governance mechanisms.

Structure is what allows leadership to scale without multiplying stress.

Why Effort Is a Poor Substitute for Structure

When structure is weak, leaders compensate with effort. They stay late. They intervene constantly. They solve problems personally.

This feels noble. It is unsustainable.

Effort is personal. Structure is transferable.

Effort expires. Structure endures.

The Test of Structural Support

A simple diagnostic question reveals whether structure exists:

If I stepped away for thirty days, what would fail first?

Whatever collapses reveals where structure is missing.

Leaders who cannot step away without disruption have not built support. They have centralized survival.

Support Must Precede Scale

Scaling before support creates dependency. Support before scale creates sustainability.

This ordering matters.

When leaders scale without support:

Quality declines, morale erodes, errors multiply, and leaders become permanent firefighters.

When leaders build support first: systems absorb growth, people develop capacity, and leadership becomes generative rather than reactive.

Why Support Feels Slow—but Isn't

Building support requires:

i.   Explanation

ii. Repetition

iii. Correction

iv. Patience

It feels slower than doing it yourself.

But every hour invested in support saves dozens later. Every system built prevents repeated crisis. Every empowered leader reduces dependency.

Support accelerates growth—after it stabilizes structure.

A Leadership Reality Few Accept

You cannot build capacity for eight billion people. You are not designed to.

Support exists because leadership is limited. **Acknowledging limitation is not failure. It is wisdom.**

Capacity expands not by removing limits—but by designing around them.

What Support Produces When Done Correctly

When relational and structural support are in place:

i.   Leaders are no longer bottlenecks

ii. Decisions flow without distortion

iii. People grow instead of waiting

iv. Systems carry pressure without collapse.

This is not loss of control. It is mature leadership.

Step Four redistributed weight.

Responsibility is no longer centralized. Support now carries what effort once sustained.

Only one step remains in the workflow: *Accountability and Review.*

Because even strong structures drift without inspection.

Step Five: Review, Reinforce, and Sustain Capacity

Why Capacity Decays Without Oversight

One of the most dangerous assumptions leaders make is this: once capacity is built, it will remain intact.

It will not.

Capacity is not static. It is dynamic, responsive, and vulnerable to drift.

Architecture teaches that structures fail more often from neglect than from sudden shock. The same is true of leadership capacity. What once held weight can weaken quietly if it is not inspected, reinforced, and recalibrated over time.

This is why capacity-building does not end with design. It ends with governance.

Capacity Requires Maintenance, Not Just Momentum

Momentum creates movement. Maintenance creates longevity.

Leaders who rely on momentum eventually confuse speed with stability. Things appear to be working, until they aren't. Cracks form slowly. Stress redistributes unevenly. Small failures are absorbed silently.

Capacity failure rarely announces itself. It erodes.

Review is how leaders detect erosion before collapse.

Why Review Feels Optional—and Isn't

Review often feels unnecessary when: outcomes are positive, growth is visible, people appear engaged, and systems seem functional.

This is precisely when review matters most.

When leaders wait for crisis to review capacity, they are already too late. Review is not corrective. It is preventive.

What Review Actually Means

Review is not micromanagement. It is not surveillance. It is not suspicion.

Review is structural awareness.

It asks:

i.   Is this still holding the weight it was designed for?

ii. Has responsibility increased without redesign?

iii. Are strain points emerging quietly?

iv. Are leaders compensating with effort again?

v.   Has urgency replaced rhythm?

Review brings reality back into focus.

Three Areas That Must Be Reviewed Regularly

Capacity review must occur across three domains: structure, people, and self.

Ignoring any of the three creates imbalance.

Structural review examines whether systems still carry responsibility without distortion. Key questions include:

i.   Are decisions flowing or bottlenecking?

ii. Are roles clear, or overlapping and confused?

iii. Are processes followed, or bypassed under pressure?

iv. Are systems supporting leaders, or consuming them?

When structure weakens, leaders compensate. That compensation masks failure—until it doesn't.

Structural review prevents leaders from becoming invisible scaffolding.

Reviewing Relational Capacity

Relational review assesses the health of trust, clarity, and shared responsibility.

Leaders must ask:

i.   Are people empowered, or waiting?

ii. Is accountability consistent, or selective?

iii. Are conflicts addressed, or avoided?

iv. Is collaboration functional, or forced?

Relational strain is often normalized because it feels personal. It is not. It is architectural.

Unaddressed relational strain eventually becomes structural failure.

Reviewing Personal Capacity

Leaders often review everything except themselves.

This is dangerous.

Personal capacity review includes:

i.   Emotional regulation under pressure

ii. Decision fatigue

iii. Boundary erosion

iv. Moral exhaustion

v.   Diminishing clarity.

Leaders who do not review themselves begin to leak pressure onto others, subtly at first, then destructively.

Self-review is not self-criticism. It is stewardship.

Reinforcement: Strengthening What Is Already Working

Review alone is insufficient. What is identified must be reinforced.

Reinforcement means adjusting systems before they fail, strengthening roles before overload, rebalancing responsibility before resentment, and restoring rhythm before burnout.

This step prevents leaders from rebuilding from collapse. It allows them to build from stability.

Why Reinforcement Is Often Resisted

Reinforcement feels inefficient. It revisits things that "already work."

But reinforcement is what keeps things working.

Leaders who resist reinforcement often: equate adjustment with regression, mistake recalibration for weakness, or fear that slowing down will cost momentum.

Reinforcement protects momentum by preserving structure.

Sustaining Capacity Over Time

Sustainability is not achieved by intensity. It is achieved by rhythm.

Capacity is sustained through: consistent review cycles, predictable accountability, rest built into systems, and clear escalation paths.

Leaders who sustain capacity do not rely on willpower. They rely on design.

A Critical Leadership Distinction

Effort sustains outcomes short-term. Structure sustains outcomes long-term.

Capacity collapses when leaders revert to effort after structure is built.

This is why review matters. It prevents regression.

When Capacity Is Sustained, Leadership Changes

When capacity is properly reviewed and reinforced: leaders stop firefighting, urgency decreases, decisions stabilize, and leadership becomes anticipatory rather than reactive.

This is maturity. Not ambition. Not charisma. Not speed.

The Final Truth of the Workflow

Capacity is not built once. It is built, reviewed, reinforced, and sustained.

Skipping the final step does not undo the work immediately. It simply delays the failure.

This workflow exists to prevent that delay from becoming collapse.

Without delegation, strength becomes the system's limitation. Not because the leader fails, but because no human capacity is designed to scale indefinitely without distribution

Dr. Joke Solanke

CHAPTER 10

◆————————◆

Delegation, Collaboration, and Governance

—

You do not have everything—even though you have many things.

When Greatness Becomes a Bottleneck

H e was one of the most influential leaders of his generation. Few names carried as much authority. Few voices commanded as much attention.

He was not an ordinary leader. His effectiveness was amplified by extraordinary abilities—insight, courage, and what many would describe as supernatural advantage. He confronted kings without apology. He shaped the destiny of an entire nation. His presence altered outcomes.

From a distance, he appeared complete—almost invincible. All-knowing. All-capable. Unchallenged.

Only a handful of people dared confront him. Fewer still survived the consequences of doing so.

And yet, the most important confrontation of his leadership did not come from an enemy, a critic, or a rival. It came from someone close. Someone who knew him well. Someone with enough authority, wisdom, and relational access to speak truth without flattery.

This individual—his former employer and one of the few who could look him in the eye without fear—made a devastatingly clear assessment:

"You are a great leader. What you do, you do well. But from a professional assessment, you do not have everything—even though you have many things.

You are setting yourself up for premature collapse—not because your time has come, but because you do not know how to build capacity."

The issue was not competence. It was not calling. It was not vision.

It was architecture.

One person attempting to personally carry the needs of millions is not heroic—it is unsustainable.

The Cost of Undistributed Strength

What made this leader exceptional also made him vulnerable.

He was accessible. He was decisive. He cared deeply. He responded personally to the needs of the people.

And because he could, he did.

But strength without distribution always produces strain.

Privately, the symptoms were already present: chronic sleep deprivation, emotional exhaustion, compromised family time, relentless pressure without recovery.

What looked like sacrifice was actually a warning.

Capacity was collapsing inward.

The Intervention That Changed Everything

What separates great leaders from broken ones is not flawlessness—it is humility under correction.

This leader listened.

He acknowledged the cost. He admitted the strain. He accepted that effectiveness had outpaced sustainability.

And then he did something that preserved his leadership rather than destroying it:

He submitted to coaching.

Not coaching on vision. Not coaching on charisma. But coaching on delegation and governance.

Delegation as a Leadership System, Not a Personality Trait

The counsel he received was not emotional. It was structural.

Delegation, he was taught, is not abdication. It is intentional architecture.

The framework was clear:

Identify people fit for responsibility not loyal alone. Not familiar alone. Fit includes competence, character, and capacity.

Assign responsibility by scope Not everything requires the same level of authority. Weight must match structure.

Establish clear reporting lines Hierarchy is not oppression. It is clarity.

Train leaders, not helpers Capacity is multiplied by leadership development, not task dumping.

Empower real authority Responsibility without authority is cruelty. Authority without accountability is chaos.

Create layers of leadership Scale requires distribution. One leader cannot be the access point for everyone.

This was not delegation as convenience. It was delegation as capacity preservation.

The Moment Leadership Stops Being Personal

This story exposes a hard truth many leaders resist:

If leadership only works when you are present, capacity has not been built—only compensated for. What made this leader extraordinary did not change. What changed was how responsibility was carried.

Delegation did not reduce influence. It multiplied it.

Delegation did not weaken authority. It stabilized it.

Delegation did not make leadership impersonal. It made it sustainable.

Why Strong Leaders Become the Ceiling

This is the paradox.

The stronger the leader, the greater the temptation to centralize responsibility.

Competence invites dependency. Availability creates reliance. Effectiveness attracts overload.

Without delegation, strength becomes the system's limitation. Not because the leader fails, but because no human capacity is designed to scale indefinitely without distribution.

The Leadership Question This Chapter Answers

This chapter is not asking, *Are you capable?*

It is asking, How *much of the system depends on you to function?*

Because that answer reveals whether leadership is built or merely holding.

Delegation is the first structural defense against leadership collapse. But delegation alone is not enough.

Delegation distributes responsibility within a system. Collaboration expands capacity beyond it.

Yet collaboration introduces its own challenges. Ego. Superiority complexes. Control issues. Fear of irrelevance. The illusion of self-sufficiency.

That is where we turn next.

Collaboration Begins Where Stewardship Is Understood

Everything she needed to change her situation was already in her possession.

It did not look impressive. It did not feel sufficient. It did not resemble the solution she was hoping for.

Yet it was enough.

That reality is uncomfortable for many people—and that is precisely why the story matters.

What stalled her progress was not absence. It was perception.

She believed the answer to her crisis had to come from outside, from something bigger, newer, and more dramatic. She did not recognize the value of what she already held because it did not match her expectation of deliverance.

And so, she did what many people still do today: she searched for a solution that did not exist, while neglecting the one that did.

This pattern repeats itself relentlessly across history.

The Illusion of Lack

We often attribute poverty, stagnation, and failure to external forces: lack of opportunity, lack of capital, lack of access, lack of connections.

While those factors matter, they are not always decisive.

In many cases, stagnation persists not because people were designed to remain small, but because they were never taught how to steward the little.

Life, by design, does not begin at scale. It never has.

Nothing in creation starts large. Seeds precede forests. Ideas precede institutions. Relationships precede movements.

Growth is not introduced through replacement. It is introduced through multiplication—and multiplication begins with stewardship.

Why Collaboration Is Often Missed

What she lacked was not oil. It was vessels.

Not more of the same resource—but capacity to contain, distribute, and sustain it.

This is where collaboration enters the conversation.

Collaboration is not about finding more. It is about creating space.

More space for ideas. More space for people. More space for systems to carry what already exists.

Many leaders fail to collaborate not because they are arrogant, but because they misunderstand where increase comes from. They assume collaboration diminishes ownership. Collaboration expands capacity.

The Role of a Mentor: Bridging the Known and the Unknown

One recurring theme in every lasting transformation story is this: someone stands between what is known and what is possible. A mentor. A guide. A voice with perspective.

Not someone who brings the solution—but someone who helps reveal it.

This is a critical leadership principle: mentorship does not add substance; it clarifies structure.

She did not receive new oil. She received new instruction.

That instruction bridged the gap between what she possessed and what she could sustain.

Collaboration often begins this way, not with consensus, but with insight.

Why Leaders Resist Collaboration

For leaders, collaboration introduces a deeper challenge than logistics.

It threatens identity.

Collaboration forces leaders to confront three uncomfortable truths:

Every human being is limited

No matter how brilliant.

No matter how popular.

No matter how successful.

No one knows everyone.

Influence is contextual.

Visibility is fragmented.

Reach is finite.

Past success does not eliminate future dependence. In fact, it often increases it.

This is where superiority complexes, inflated ego, and subtle forms of self-sufficiency emerge—especially after repeated success.

Human admiration can become dangerous. When people begin to rely on you excessively, it feels validating—but it erodes systems.

This is why some leaders unconsciously resist collaboration: collaboration interrupts heroism.

But leadership was never designed to be heroic. It was designed to be sustainable.

Collaboration Is Not Duplication

Many leaders believe collaboration means finding people who think like them, act like them, and reproduce their methods. That is not collaboration—it is replication.

Replication is fragile. Collaboration is resilient.

Collaboration embraces difference, different temperaments, different skill sets, different perspectives, different access points.

This is how capacity multiplies.

What she needed were vessels—not copies of her oil.

Likewise, leaders do not scale by cloning themselves. They scale by building complementary systems.

Stewardship before Scale

The most overlooked leadership principle is this:

You cannot scale what you cannot steward.

Collaboration without stewardship creates chaos. Stewardship without collaboration creates limitation.

The order matters.

She had oil. She needed vessels. And she needed instruction to use both together.

That sequence is not incidental. It is architectural.

Why This Matters for Capacity

Capacity is not increased by accumulation. It is increased by containment.

Collaboration creates containment.

Governance stabilizes it.

Delegation distributes it.

Without collaboration: leaders hoard responsibility, systems depend on personality, and growth remains fragile.

With collaboration: capacity expands beyond the individual, impact becomes repeatable, and leadership outlives presence.

A Leadership Reality Worth Facing

Many leaders are exhausted not because they are doing too much, but because they are doing too much alone.

They have oil. They lack vessels.

They have insight. They lack structure.

They have vision. They lack collaboration.

And often, what they need most is not another breakthrough, but another perspective.

Delegation distributes responsibility within a system. Collaboration expands capacity across systems.

But collaboration without governance creates confusion. And governance without delegation creates control.

In the next section, we examine how governance protects collaboration, and why accountability beyond self is the final safeguard against leadership collapse.

Governance Begins With Values: Why Capacity Without Order Collapses

Governance is often misunderstood as restriction—rules, oversight, enforcement, and control. Governance is not about limiting people. It is about protecting purpose.

Governance becomes necessary the moment responsibility exceeds intuition.

As long as leadership remains small, informal, and proximity-based, values can remain implicit. People intuitively understand what matters. Decisions are relational. Corrections are conversational. Accountability is personal.

But scale breaks informality. When people multiply, when distance increases, when responsibility expands beyond direct supervision, assumptions fail. What was once understood must now be articulated. What was once relational must now be structural.

This is where governance begins.

Why Governance Is Impossible Without Values

Governance answers one foundational question:

By what standard will decisions be made when the leader is not present?

That question cannot be answered by personality. It cannot be answered by charisma. It cannot be answered by goodwill.

It can only be answered by clearly defined values and guiding principles.

Values are not inspirational statements. They are decision filters.

Guiding principles are not motivational slogans.
They are behavioral boundaries.

Without them:

i.   Delegation becomes risky

ii. Collaboration becomes chaotic

iii. Accountability becomes personal

iv. Enforcement becomes inconsistent.

Governance is easy when direction is clear. It is nearly impossible when the heart of the vision is vague.

Moses and the Necessity of Codified Principles (Extracted, Not Quoted)

Moses' leadership challenge was not spiritual, it was structural.

He was leading a population too large for personality-based leadership. Proximity was impossible. Direct access was unsustainable. Decision-making had become centralized, exhausting, and inefficient.

The solution was not more effort. It was codification.

What the Ten Commandments represented, stripped of religious framing, was a rule of law:

i.   Shared standards

ii. Agreed boundaries

iii. Non-negotiable principles,

And a framework that governed behavior independent of the leader's presence.

This was not about control. It was about order.

The principles created:

i.   Predictability

ii. Fairness

iii. Consistency

iv. Transferability.

Leadership shifted from reactive arbitration to principled governance.

That is capacity at scale.

Governance Is Not Limited to Government

One of the most damaging misconceptions about governance is that it applies only to nations or political systems.

Governance exists everywhere capacity exists.

Individuals govern themselves through values, boundaries, and discipline.

Teams govern behavior through norms, roles, and expectations.

Organizations govern operations through policies, ethics, and accountability systems.

Institutions govern continuity through culture, succession, and codified purpose.

Where governance is absent, personality fills the gap. Where personality dominates, sustainability erodes.

This is why organizations collapse after founders leave. This is why families repeat cycles. This is why teams function only under pressure. This is why leaders become bottlenecks.

Governance was never built.

Core Values as Structural Anchors

Values are often treated as cultural accessories. They are load-bearing elements.

They determine:

i.   What is rewarded?

ii. What is tolerated?

iii. What is corrected?

iv. What is protected.

Without explicit values:

i. Decisions feel arbitrary

ii. Accountability feels personal

iii. And trust erodes.

With clear values:

i. Decisions feel consistent

ii. Accountability feels fair

iii. And delegation becomes safe.

Values do not remove conflict. They frame it.

Guiding principles do not eliminate tension. They stabilize it.

Why Systems Require Governance before Scale

Every system, whether personal, relational, or institutional, eventually reaches a point where intentions are no longer sufficient.

At that point:

i. Memory fails

ii. Interpretation varies

iii. And alignment fractures

Governance transforms intention into infrastructure.

It answers:

Who decides?

By what criteria?

With what authority?

And toward what end?

Without these answers, collaboration disintegrates and delegation becomes dangerous.

Governance as Protection, Not Control

True governance does not exist to restrict good people. It exists to protect the mission from human limitation.

It protects:

i.   People from favoritism

ii. Leaders from overload

iii. Systems from drift

iv. Purpose from dilution.

When governance is absent, leaders compensate with control. When governance is clear, leaders can release responsibility without fear.

This is why governance is not the enemy of collaboration. It is its safeguard.

The Capacity Link

Capacity does not scale through enthusiasm. It scales through order.

Delegation without governance creates chaos. Collaboration without values creates confusion. Authority without principles creates abuse.

But when values are clear, principles are codified, and systems are aligned, capacity multiplies without increasing pressure on the leader.

That is the goal.

If collaboration creates space, and governance creates order, then delegation determines flow.

In the next section, we examine delegation not as trust, but as architecture, and why leaders who refuse to delegate are not protecting excellence, but sabotaging sustainability.

Delegation Is Not Trust — It Is Architecture

One of the most persistent myths in leadership is the belief that delegation is primarily about trust.

It is not.

Trust is relational. Delegation is structural.

When leaders frame delegation as trust, they personalize it. They delegate based on comfort, loyalty, familiarity, or emotional safety. When trust is broken, or perceived to be broken, delegation collapses, and responsibility rushes back to the leader.

This is why so many leaders say:

"I can't delegate because no one will do it like I do."

"I tried delegating before, and it failed."

"I trust very few people."

These statements sound relational, but they reveal a structural problem.

Delegation failed not because people were untrustworthy, but because architecture was absent.

Why Trust-Based Delegation Fails

Trust-based delegation assumes:

i. People will interpret expectations correctly

ii. Alignment will persist without structure

iii. Accountability will emerge naturally

iv. Outcomes will self-correct.

That assumption is fragile.

Trust can motivate effort. It cannot carry complexity. When delegation is built on trust alone:

i. Roles blur

ii. Authority overlaps

iii. Accountability becomes personal

iv. Correction feels relationally threatening.

Leaders then step back in, not because delegation was wrong, but because it was unframed.

Delegation without architecture creates anxiety for everyone involved.

Architectural Delegation Creates Clarity

Architectural delegation asks different questions:

What decisions belong where?

What authority accompanies responsibility?

What outcomes define success?

What feedback loops exist?

What happens when things go wrong?

These questions remove delegation from emotion and place it into design.

Delegation is not releasing work. It is redistributing load.

And load must be distributed intentionally, or it collapses back to the strongest point—which is usually the leader.

]

Why Strong Leaders Hoard Responsibility

High-capacity leaders often become accidental bottlenecks.

Not because they are insecure. Not because they are controlling. But because they are competent.

Competence attracts responsibility. Reliability accumulates weight. Excellence invites dependency.

Over time, the leader becomes the default solution.

This feels noble. It feels responsible. It feels necessary.

But it is unsustainable.

Leadership that relies on personal excellence rather than structural delegation will always cap growth.

The system grows only to the limits of the leader's stamina.

The Hidden Cost of Non-Delegation

When leaders retain responsibility instead of redesigning structure:

i. Decisions slow

ii. Teams disengage

iii. Leaders burn out

iv. Organizations become fragile.

More subtly:

i. Innovation declines

ii. Ownership disappears

iii. Initiative dies.

People stop thinking. They wait.

Not because they lack ability—but because the system trained them to.

This is not a people problem. It is a design problem.

Architectural Delegation Creates Clarity

Delegation becomes effective when it is framed architecturally:

i.   Clear roles — who owns what, without overlap

ii. Defined authority — what decisions can be made without escalation

iii. Explicit accountability — how success and failure are evaluated

iv. Feedback systems — how correction occurs without humiliation

v.   Escalation paths — when and how leadership intervenes

When these exist, trust becomes unnecessary as a prerequisite.

Trust can grow after structure, not before it.

Why Delegation Feels Risky Without Architecture

Leaders fear delegation because they fear:

i.   Reputational damage

ii. Loss of control

iii. Inconsistency

iv. Failure they cannot correct in time.

Those fears are valid only in poorly designed systems.

In a well-designed system:

i.   Failure is contained

ii. Mistakes are instructive

iii. Accountability is distributed.

Delegation stops being risky when failure no longer threatens the whole.

Architecture absorbs error. Personality does not.

Delegation Protects Capacity

Delegation is not about efficiency. It is about preservation.

It preserves:

i.   Leader energy

ii. Decision quality

iii. Emotional regulation

iv. Long-term sustainability.

Leaders who refuse to delegate often believe they are protecting excellence. They are eroding capacity—slowly and quietly.

Delegation is how leaders remain effective over time, not just in seasons of intensity.

Delegation Is Not Abdication

Architectural delegation does not mean absence.

It means:

i.   Fewer interventions

ii. Clearer boundaries

iii. Strategic presence.

Leaders remain responsible. They are no longer required to be involved in everything.

This distinction is critical.

Delegation is not stepping away. It is stepping up—into governance rather than execution.

The Capacity Test

A simple diagnostic question reveals whether delegation is architectural or emotional:

Does the system function when I am unavailable?

If the answer is no, delegation has not occurred. Responsibility has only been delayed.

True delegation creates continuity without proximity.

If delegation distributes weight, and governance provides order, then teams determine scale.

The next section explores how teams function as capacity multipliers—and why leadership that remains individual, no matter how brilliant, will always remain limited.

How Teams Function as Capacity Multipliers

Delegation redistributes weight. Teams multiply capacity.

This distinction matters.

A leader can delegate tasks and remain the ceiling of the organization. *Capacity is not multiplied simply because work is assigned to others. Capacity is multiplied when systems of people carry different dimensions of responsibility simultaneously, without competing for authority or collapsing into chaos.*

Teams are not useful because there are many people. They are powerful because no single person carries the whole load.

Capacity Multiplies When Load Is Distributed, Not Duplicated

Most leaders build teams incorrectly.

They look for replicas:

i.   People who think like them

ii.   Work like them

iii. Solve problems like them

iv.   Validate their approach.

This feels efficient. It is fragile.

Replication duplicates effort. It does not multiply capacity.

True teams distribute different kinds of weight across different people.

One carries strategy. Another carries execution. Another carries relational stability. Another carries detail and continuity. Another carries innovation and disruption.

Capacity multiplies not through sameness, but through complementarity.

Why Individual Excellence Does Not Scale

Individual excellence is linear.

No matter how gifted a leader is:

i.   One mind processes one stream of thought at a time

ii. One body occupies one location

iii. One emotional system absorbs only so much pressure.

Excellence increases performance. It does not increase bandwidth.

Teams create bandwidth. They allow:

i.   Parallel processing of decisions

ii. Simultaneous problem-solving

iii. Sustained functioning under pressure.

This is why organizations built around "exceptional individuals" always plateau. They hit the limits of human capacity.

Teams are not about help. They are about structure.

The Multiplication Effect: Parallel Responsibility

Teams multiply capacity by enabling parallel responsibility.

This means:

i.   Decisions are made simultaneously at multiple levels

ii. Issues are resolved closer to where they arise

iii. Leadership presence is no longer required everywhere at once.

When responsibility remains centralized, leaders become traffic controllers. When responsibility is distributed, leaders become system stewards.

Multiplication happens when:

i.   Authority matches responsibility

ii. Clarity replaces permission

iii. Accountability is localized.

This is why teams without authority still fail. They are busy, but not powerful.

Why Teams Fail to Multiply Capacity

Teams fail when they are assembled for optics rather than architecture.

Common failure patterns include:

i.   Unclear roles

ii. Overlapping authority

iii. Decision ambiguity

iv. Emotional competition

v.   Unspoken power hierarchies.

When these exist, teams do not multiply capacity. They increase friction.

The leader ends up mediating constantly. Work slows. Energy drains. Delegation collapses back upward.

The team becomes a meeting. Not a multiplier.

Teams Multiply Capacity When Structure Is Clear

Effective teams share several structural characteristics:

Clear Domains of Ownership

Each member knows:

i. What they own

ii. What they influence

iii. What they do not touch.

Decision Authority Is Explicit

People do not wait for approval unnecessarily. They act within defined boundaries.

Accountability is role-based, not personal

Correction is not an attack. Feedback is not emotional. Performance is measured against structure, not loyalty.

Conflict Is Functional, Not Personal

Differences are expected. Tension is processed. Disagreement improves outcomes rather than destabilizing relationships.

When these are present, teams carry weight the leader no longer has to.

Teams Absorb Pressure Leaders Cannot

One of the least discussed functions of teams is pressure absorption.

Without teams:

i.   Every failure land on the leader

ii. Every conflict escalates upward,

iii. Every decision requires central approval.

With teams:

i.   Pressure is dispersed

ii. Conflict is resolved at appropriate levels

iii. Emotional load is shared.

This does not weaken leadership. It preserves it.

Leaders who refuse to build teams often believe they are being responsible. They are becoming shock absorbers for the entire system.

That is not strength. That is fragility.

Teams Allow Leadership to Shift from Presence to Design

At scale, leadership must transition from presence to design.

If outcomes depend on:

i.   Who is in the room?

ii. Who is watching?

iii. Who is intervening,

Capacity has not been multiplied.

Teams allow leaders to step back without collapse. They create continuity without supervision. They enable progress without constant correction.

This is the difference between:

Leadership as activity,

And leadership as architecture.

Why Teams Are a Test of Leader Maturity

Teams expose leaders.

They reveal:

i.   Ego maturity

ii. Insecurity

iii. Need for control

iv. Tolerance for difference.

Leaders who require validation struggle with teams.

Leaders who equate authority with dominance sabotage them.

Leaders who fear being replaced resist multiplication.

But leaders who understand capacity welcome teams, not as competition, but as reinforcement.

Teams do not diminish influence. They extend it.

Capacity Multiplies When Leaders Let Go of Centrality

The most difficult transition for strong leaders is releasing centrality.

Not responsibility. Centrality.

This means:

Not being copied on everything

Not being consulted on every decision

Not being the emotional center of the system

This feels like loss. It is freedom.

When leaders release centrality: innovation increases, decision speed improves, and sustainability emerges.

This is when leadership stops being exhausting.

A Diagnostic Question

To determine whether your teams are multiplying capacity or merely assisting, ask:

If I step away for thirty days, does the system stabilize, stall, or collapse?

Stability indicates multiplication. Stalling indicates partial delegation. Collapse indicates dependence.

This is not about worth. It is about design.

Teams multiply capacity. Governance protects it.

Without governance, teams fragment. Without teams, governance centralizes. Without both, leaders become the ceiling.

Collaboration, Networking, and the Myth of the Self-Sufficient Leader

Teams multiply capacity internally. Collaboration and networking extend capacity externally.

Many leaders confuse these two—and as a result, they isolate themselves at the very moment scale requires expansion.

Collaboration is not weakness. Networking is not opportunism. Both are acknowledgments of a fundamental truth:

No individual, no matter how brilliant, gifted, or successful, has sufficient reach, insight, or access alone.

Capacity does not grow by accumulation. It grows by connection.

Why Collaboration Is a Capacity Issue, Not a Personality Preference

Some leaders avoid collaboration because of temperament. Others because of past betrayal. Still others because success has conditioned them to trust only themselves.

But collaboration is not about liking people. It is about recognizing limitation. *Every leader is limited by: time, geography, perspective, expertise, and access.*

Collaboration is how leaders extend beyond those limits without overextension.

Refusing to collaborate does not preserve strength. It concentrates fragility.

Networking Is Not About Visibility — It Is About Coverage

Networking is often reduced to branding, influence, or social capital. That is shallow and unsustainable.

Networking is capacity mapping.

It answers questions like:

Who holds insight I do not?

Who operates in spaces I cannot reach?

Who understands systems I am unfamiliar with?

Who can open doors my excellence cannot?

No matter how accomplished you are, not everyone knows you. Not every system responds to your credentials. Not every door opens to your reputation.

Networking is how leaders extend influence without forcing presence.

Why High-Achieving Leaders Struggle With Collaboration

The leaders who struggle most with collaboration are often the most accomplished.

Repeated success creates a dangerous illusion: "If it worked because of me before, it would always work because of me."

This is the birthplace of hero syndrome.

Hero syndrome is not arrogance. It is over-identification with success.

It develops when: results consistently depend on one person, organizations reward personal heroics, and leaders are praised for being indispensable.

Over time, indispensability becomes identity.

Super-Ego and the Collapse of Scale

Super-ego in leadership does not always look like pride. Sometimes it looks like responsibility.

"I can't delegate this."

"No one else will do it right."

"It's faster if I handle it."

"They're not ready yet."

These statements sound reasonable. They are architectural warnings.

Super-ego leadership centralizes everything: decisions, knowledge, access, and authority.

This feels powerful. It is actually brittle.

The more successful the leader, the more damaging this becomes, because success attracts more weight.

Eventually: collaboration is avoided, networking feels unnecessary, and the leader becomes the system.

That system cannot scale.

The Cost of Hero Leadership

Hero leadership always produces the same outcomes: leaders become exhausted, teams become passive, innovation slows, succession is impossible, and collapse follows transition.

Not because the leader was wrong. But because the structure depended on a single point of failure.

Hero leadership builds monuments. Capacity leadership builds ecosystems.

Collaboration as Distributed Intelligence

Collaboration works because intelligence is distributed, not centralized.

No leader sees everything. No perspective is complete. No experience covers all contingencies.

When leaders collaborate, blind spots are reduced, decisions improve, and risk is shared.

Collaboration does not dilute authority. It refines judgment.

This is why mature leaders seek voices that challenge them, not flatter them.

Networking without Dependency

Healthy networking does not create dependency. It creates interdependence.

This means: you are not trying to be everywhere, you are not outsourcing responsibility, and you are not surrendering vision.

You are building relational infrastructure that allows movement, influence, and exchange without personal overextension.

Networking becomes dangerous only when leaders use it to compensate for internal deficiency. When used correctly, it extends already-built capacity.

A Diagnostic Question for Leaders Ask yourself:

Am I surrounded by people who expand my thinking—or only by people who affirm my competence?

Affirmation feels good. Expansion builds capacity.

If collaboration feels threatening, ego, not vision, is likely in control.

From Hero to Host

The most sustainable leaders make a quiet but profound shift:

They move from hero to host.

Heroes perform. Hosts design environments where others perform.

Heroes are remembered. Hosts are reproduced.

This shift marks the transition from leadership as achievement to leadership as architecture.

Delegation, Teams, Collaboration, and Governance: How Capacity Multiplies and Endures

Leadership fails most often not because leaders lack vision, intelligence, or drive—but because they attempt to scale responsibility with structures designed for smaller weight.

This chapter has reframed delegation, teams, collaboration, and governance not as interpersonal preferences or trust exercises, but as architectural necessities.

Delegation is not about believing in people. It is about redistributing load, so the system does not collapse.

Teams are not about inclusion. They are about parallel responsibility and sustained function.

Collaboration and networking are not about visibility. They are about extending capacity beyond personal limitation.

Governance is not about control. It is about preserving mission, people, and continuity when leadership scales beyond personality.

At every point, the danger is the same: when leaders confuse personal excellence with systemic sufficiency, they become the ceiling they were meant to remove.

Hero leadership may produce moments of brilliance. Architectural leadership produces longevity.

The mature leader eventually accepts a sobering truth:

If everything still depends on me, capacity has not been built— only compensated for.

> *True capacity is visible when leadership works without constant presence, decisions are made without fear, and progress continues without heroics.*

This is not a loss of influence. It is the highest expression of it.

With this foundation established, the next chapter turns inward again, not to personality, but to process, to examine how capacity is built deliberately through design rather than hope.

*The very capacity you build to access
more will expose you to pressures you
never faced before.*

Dr. Joke Solanke

CHAPTER 11

◆————————————◆

Capacity under pressure

——

C apacity is proven when conditions deteriorate. Life is designed with pressure built into it.

Pressure is not an interruption of life; it is woven into its fabric. It is not a matter of if pressure will come, but when. This is one of the most predictable realities of existence. Growth, responsibility, opportunity, relationships, leadership—all attract pressure as a natural consequence.

Pressure arrives with both good and not-so-good experiences. Expansion brings possibility, but it also brings strain. Influence opens doors, but it also exposes vulnerabilities. Capacity, once built, does not lead to ease—it leads to more weight.

This is where many people misunderstand life, leadership, and success. They assume that capacity is meant to reduce pressure. It does not. Capacity increases your ability to carry pressure without collapse, not your exemption from it.

If you live in tropical regions, strong winds are not optional. They are not anomalies. They are predictable. Structures are not built hoping storms won't come; they are built because storms will come.

Leadership, influence, and responsibility function the same way.

Pressure is predictable. Failure under pressure is optional.

Most leaders misunderstand pressure. They assume pressure is the enemy, something to be avoided, escaped, or prayed away. In reality, pressure is diagnostic. It exposes the true strength of what has already been built.

A structure that collapses under pressure was not betrayed by pressure. It was revealed by it.

This chapter explores how capacity behaves when conditions deteriorate—when clarity is reduced, stakes are elevated, and margin disappears. These are the moments where leadership is no longer theoretical and systems can no longer hide behind routine.

Why Pressure Is Not the Enemy

Pressure does not destroy strong structures. It reveals weak ones.

Most failures blamed on pressure are actually failures of preparation. Pressure only exposes what was already insufficient. A bridge that collapses under load did not fail because traffic was unfair, it failed because the structure was inadequate for what it was designed to carry.

In life and leadership, pressure reveals emotional maturity, ethical alignment, relational discipline, internal boundaries, and decision-making architecture.

Pressure does not ask what you believe. It asks what you've built.

The Myth of Immunity

One of the most dangerous illusions leaders carry is the belief that intelligence, spirituality, wisdom, or past success will immunize them against pressure.

It will not.

Emotional pressure has destroyed giants.

I remember a very brilliant CEO—exceptional business acumen, strategic clarity, strong public credibility. His downfall was not incompetence. It was emotional incapacity. He could not withstand sustained emotional pressure exerted by someone far beneath him in hierarchy, an intern.

That pressure cost him his marriage. It cost him his reputation. It ultimately cost him his position.

Capacity failure rarely announces itself loudly. It begins with unguarded exposure.

Capacity Opens Access—Pressure Follows

One of the cruel ironies of life is this:

The very capacity you build to access more will expose you to pressures you never faced before.

At lower levels of responsibility, pressure is limited and contained. At higher levels, pressure becomes:

i. Relational

ii. Emotional

iii. Ethical

iv. Reputational

v. Systemic.

Capacity does not remove you from people, it pushes you into proximity with them.

Moses was comfortable with God alone. Capacity forced him into the chaos of people. He was prepared for divine encounters, but people pressure stretched him in ways solitude never could.

This is where many leaders falter.

They are prepared for success. They are not prepared for exposure.

Pressure strips leadership down to its architecture.

Why Pressure Is the Truest Test of Capacity

In stable conditions, many weaknesses remain invisible. Effort compensates. Personality smooths edges. Momentum covers cracks. But pressure compresses time, emotion, and consequence simultaneously.

Under pressure: decisions must be made faster, errors cost more, tolerance for ambiguity shrinks, and emotional regulation is tested.

What leaders say they value matters less than what they default to. What they intend matters less than what their structure allows.

Pressure does not ask what you believe. It asks what you've built.

The Sources of Pressure Leaders Must Anticipate

Pressure is not random. It arrives through identifiable channels. Leaders who fail under pressure often do so not because pressure was excessive, but because its source was misunderstood.

Capacity cannot be evaluated without understanding where pressure comes from.

Growth Pressure

Growth is one of the most deceptive forms of pressure because it looks like success.

Growth introduces complexity, visibility, decision density, and reduced margin for error.

Growth does not stabilize weak structures. It magnifies them.

Many leadership failures occur after expansion, not before it. Growth asks a sobering question:

Can this structure carry more of itself?

When the answer is no, growth becomes acceleration toward collapse.

Unplanned Pressure

Some pressure arrives without invitation: crisis, health disruption, economic instability, regulatory change, or leadership gaps.

Unplanned pressure is dangerous because it demands immediate capacity.

There is no time to build when it arrives. Only what already exists can be deployed.

Unplanned pressure exposes whether leadership strength was situational or structural.

Opportunity Pressure

Sudden opportunity is rarely recognized as pressure—until it overwhelms.

People who win the lottery often return to previous financial states, not because money disappeared, but because their internal and structural capacity was never built to sustain it.

The same principle applies to leadership: unexpected promotion, rapid influence, sudden funding, or public visibility.

Opportunity does not upgrade capacity. It reveals it.

People Pressure

As leadership expands, so does relational weight: expectations multiply, misinterpretations increase, dependency intensifies, and emotional exposure deepens.

Leaders often say, "The work isn't the problem—the people are." In reality, ungoverned people systems are the pressure source.

People pressure cannot be eliminated. It must be distributed and structured.

Capacity must include emotional regulation, boundaries, and governance, or people pressure will erode even the strongest vision.

Internal Pressure

The most destructive pressure often comes from within perfectionism, fear of failure, identity attachment to success, comparison, or unresolved trauma.

Internal pressure fuels: chronic urgency, over-functioning, control, and burnout mislabeled as dedication.

Leaders often collapse not under external demand, but under self-generated pressure.

The Illusion of Competence in Calm Seasons

Some leaders appear exceptional—until pressure arrives.

This is not because they were fraudulent. It is because calm conditions allowed: over-functioning, informal problem-solving, personality-driven leadership, and reactive decision-making to masquerade as capacity.

When pressure arrives, these compensations collapse.

Calm seasons reward agility. Pressure seasons demand architecture.

Decision Fatigue:

When Capacity Is Eroded by Volume

One of the first signs of capacity strain under pressure is decision fatigue.

Decision fatigue occurs when leaders are required to make too many decisions that should already be resolved by structure.

Symptoms include delayed decisions, impulsive reversals, avoidance disguised as discernment, or emotional decision-making.

Decision fatigue is not a time-management issue. It is a governance issue.

High-capacity leaders do not make better decisions under pressure. They make fewer decisions—because most have already been decided in advance.

Conflict Exposure: Pressure Reveals Relational Capacity

Pressure accelerates conflict. It does not create it.

Under strain: unspoken tensions surface, weak trust fractures, resentment erupts, and misalignment becomes unavoidable.

Low relational capacity produces personalization, domination, or avoidance.

High relational capacity produces steadiness, clarity, and regulation.

Pressure does not reward charisma. It rewards regulation.

Crisis Moments: When Structure Is Activated or Exposed

Crisis is pressure with consequence.

In crisis: information is incomplete, timelines collapse, emotions intensify, scrutiny increases.

Leadership does not rise to the occasion. It defaults to its deepest habits.

Improvisation feels powerful—until it fails repeatedly.

Emotional Endurance: Carrying Weight without Distortion

Pressure introduces prolonged emotional weight.

Leaders without endurance discharge stress, withdraw, numb, or seek validation. Leaders with endurance process emotion without leakage.

This is not temperament. It is trained capacity.

Recovery Speed: The Most Overlooked Indicator of Capacity

Everyone is affected by pressure. Capacity determines how quickly function is restored.

Low-capacity systems replay damage. High-capacity systems stabilize, repair, and return to baseline.

Capacity is not about avoiding disruption. It is about minimizing residual damage.

Why Leaders Break Under Pressure

Leaders break not because pressure is excessive, but because: capacity was assumed instead of built, systems were deferred for speed, governance was postponed, and emotional regulation was never trained.

Pressure does not arrive unexpectedly. It arrives eventually.

Capacity under Pressure Is Built Before Pressure Arrives

This is the sobering truth of leadership:

Capacity cannot be installed during crisis. Pressure is not the moment of construction. It is the moment of testing.

Pressure did not break the leader. It revealed what had not been built.

Pressure Is Predictable—Guardrails Are Not Optional

If pressure is inevitable, then the most important question is not how I avoid it, but:

What guardrails must exist before pressure arrives?

Guardrails are not reactions. They are pre-decisions.

They include ethical boundaries that do not shift under opportunity, relational accountability that is not based on admiration, emotional self-awareness, policies that protect you from yourself, and systems that restrict access before temptation appears.

Many leaders attempt to install guardrails after pressure intensifies. That is always too late.

Capacity must be paired with restraint.

Pressure Is Not a Sign You're off Course

This is critical:

Pressure is not proof you missed God. Pressure is not proof you chose wrongly. Pressure is not proof you are failing.

Pressure is proof you are carrying weight.

The question is not whether pressure exists. The question is whether your capacity can hold it without distortion.

The Real Test of Capacity

Capacity under pressure is not measured by: how loud you speak, how spiritual you appear, or how much you endure.

It is measured by: what collapses, what remains intact, what leaks, and what stabilizes.

Pressure reveals whether leadership is sustained by effort or supported by structure.

Life did not design pressure to destroy you. It designed pressure to expose what needs reinforcement.

Capacity is not built to escape pressure. It is built to remain whole while carrying it.

Pressure is not the enemy. Unbuilt capacity is

You can replace leaders quickly. You cannot replace culture easily. This is why institutions outlive founders. And why nations inherit consequences long after architects are gone.

—

Dr. Joke Solanke

CHAPTER 12

◆————————————————◆

Built to Carry

———

C apacity is embedded in creation's pattern.

Capacity ultimately answers a single question: What will remain functional when I am no longer present?

At earlier stages of leadership, success is often personal. It is tied to effort, gifting, insight, and momentum. But at scale—across families, institutions, and nations—success becomes collective and structural. It is no longer about who you are. It is about what you have built that can survive you.

This is where many strong people fail.

Not because they lack brilliance. Not because they lack calling. But because they are strong individuals operating inside weak systems.

Strong People in Weak Systems

History is full of gifted individuals who burned out inside fragile frameworks. Their intelligence was real. Their influence was visible. Their impact, however, was temporary.

Strong people can compensate for weak systems for a time. But compensation is not capacity.

Eventually:

i.   effort replaces structure,

ii.   heroics replace governance,

iii. urgency replaces rhythm,

iv.   personality replaces process.

And when the individual steps away—everything collapses.

Capacity at this level is not about becoming stronger. It is about building structures that do not depend on strength.

Culture as a Capacity Carrier

At the highest level, capacity is carried by culture.

Culture is what people do: when no one is watching, when pressure rises, when leadership is absent, when convenience competes with values.

Culture is invisible architecture.

It determines: how decisions are made, how power is used, how conflict is handled, how truth is preserved, how succession occurs.

You can replace leaders quickly. You cannot replace culture easily. This is why institutions outlive founders. And why nations inherit consequences long after architects are gone.

Culture is capacity that has learned how to reproduce.

Legacy vs. Impact

Impact is what happens through you. Legacy is what continues without you.

Impact is often loud. Legacy is usually quiet.

Impact excites the moment. Legacy stabilizes the future.

Many leaders confuse the two—and chase visibility when what is required is endurance.

Being built to carry means asking a harder question than "How far can I go?"

It asks:

What can survive me?

What continues to function when my presence is removed? What values remain intact under new leadership?

Capacity at this level demands restraint more than ambition.

Succession Readiness: The Final Test of Capacity

Succession is not an afterthought. It is the ultimate audit of leadership capacity.

If leadership collapses when authority transfers, capacity was never complete.

Succession readiness includes:

i. Distributed authority,

ii. Codified values,

iii. Clear governance,

iv. Leaders developed beyond dependency,

v. Systems that reward alignment, not proximity.

You are not built to carry if everything depends on you.

You are built to carry when what you built can carry others.

THE OIL OR THE VESSEL — WHERE IT ALL BEGINS

This entire book was inspired by a woman I never met.

She had oil. That was never the problem.

What she lacked was capacity—not more oil.

The solution was not duplication. It was vessels.

She was searching for something external when everything required for her next level was already in her house.

That is the quiet tragedy repeated across generations.

We look for what we already carry. We pray for increase without preparing containers. We chase solutions while ignoring structure.

Life by design never starts big. Seeds precede harvests.

Fruitfulness precedes multiplication.
Multiplication precedes replenishment.
Replenishment precedes dominion.

Capacity is embedded in creation's pattern.

Starting small is not failure.
Remaining small because you never learned capacity is.

STAYING OIL WITHOUT LOSING IMPACT

Here is the clarity many leaders never receive:
Sometimes you are not meant to become the vessel.
Sometimes all you are meant to be is oil.
And that is not inferiority.

Oil flows. Oil multiplies by contact.
Oil increases impact by connection.

Trying to become the vessel when you were designed to pour creates exhaustion and identity confusion.

Some people are builders. Others are carriers of essence.

You may never become the container but you can expand influence by aligning with the right vessels.

Oil grows by connection, not by imitation.

The mistake is trying to be everything instead of being effective.

WHAT TYPE OF VESSELS DO I NEED?

This is the wiser question.

Not: How do I become bigger?

But: What kind of vessels can carry what I already have?

Vessels may not look like you.

They may not think like you.

They may not even value what you value initially.

But they are necessary.

Oil without vessels leaks. Vessels without oil are empty.

Capacity is alignment—not sameness.

PERSONAL INVENTORY —
WHAT IS IN YOUR HOUSE?

Take a moment. Answer honestly.

i.   Am I oil, vessel, or both?

ii. Where have I tried to become a vessel when I was designed to pour?

iii. Where has my oil been leaking due to lack of structure?

iv. What vessels am I currently connected to?

v.   What vessels do I resist because they don't resemble me?

vi. Where have I mistaken isolation for independence?

vii. What capacity must be built before I seek increase?

This is not judgment. It is clarity.

APPENDIX A

◆——————————————————◆

CAPACITY READINESS ASSESSMENT

———

Before You Begin

The following diagnostic is not designed to affirm your readiness or expose deficiency. It is designed to surface structural truth.

Respond based on how your leadership functions under pressure— not how you believe it should function, or how it has functioned in the past.

If you answer aspirationally, the tool will be useless. If you answer honestly, it will be protective.

Proceed without haste. Capacity grows from clarity, not optimism.

Rating Scale

Rate each statement on a scale of 1–5:

1 — rarely true / structurally absent

2 — inconsistently true / fragile

3 — generally true / requires effort

4 — consistently true / structurally supported

5 — fully true / sustainable without heroics

Appendix A.1

Capacity Readiness Diagnostic

(Readiness before Expansion)

This diagnostic is not a personality test. It is an architectural scan. Its purpose is to assess whether your current internal and structural capacity can sustain increased responsibility without strain, compensation, or erosion.

Respond based on current reality, not aspiration. Evaluate how the system functions when you are not present.

A. Self-Awareness & Assessment Readiness

(Reality Alignment)

1. I can accurately describe my current limits without shame or defensiveness.

2. I regularly assess what I am carrying emotionally, mentally, and structurally.

3. I can identify where I am stretched versus where I am functioning sustainably.

4. I pause to evaluate before accepting additional responsibility.

5. I recognize patterns of strain before they become crises.

Score Insight: Low scores indicate growth occurring without awareness. Capacity cannot be built where reality is avoided.

B. Emotional & Mental Capacity

(Pressure Containment)

1. I remain emotionally regulated when outcomes are not in my control.

2. I tolerate ambiguity without becoming reactive or withdrawn.

3. I receive feedback without personalizing it.

4. I can hold tension or dissatisfaction without rushing resolution.

5. I recover emotionally after pressure rather than carrying it forward.

Score Insight: Low scores signal emotional fatigue that will be exposed as responsibility increases.

C. Relational & People Capacity

(Human Load Management)

1. I manage people differently than I manage tasks.

2. I can lead individuals with personalities unlike my own.

3. I do not avoid necessary difficult conversations.

4. I delegate without losing trust or resorting to control.

5. I discern when collaboration is required rather than individual effort.

Score Insight: Low scores suggest relational capacity has not kept pace with role demands.

D. Structural & Systemic Capacity

(Infrastructure Support)

1. I rely on systems more than personal effort.
2. Processes function without my constant involvement.
3. I understand how my decisions affect people beyond my immediate scope.
4. I can identify where I have become a bottleneck.
5. I actively design structures that reduce dependency on me.

Score Insight: Low scores indicate over-functioning. Growth without systems accelerates burnout.

E. Accountability & Governance Readiness

(Responsibility Expansion)

1. I accept responsibility for outcomes I did not personally cause.
2. I can make decisions that disappoint some people permanently.
3. I do not require affirmation to maintain clarity.
4. I welcome accountability rather than resisting it.
5. I understand that leadership includes restraint, not just authority.

Score Insight: Low scores signal limits in readiness for expanded authority.

F. Stamina & Sustainability

(Longevity under Load)

1. I maintain rhythms that support long-term effectiveness.
2. I rest intentionally rather than only after exhaustion.
3. I recognize early signs of burnout in myself.
4. I can carry prolonged responsibility without losing clarity.
5. I have practices that preserve effectiveness under sustained pressure.

Score Insight: Weak stamina undermines every other form of capacity.

G. Identity & Alignment

(Design Integrity)

1. I understand what I am designed to carry—and what I am not.
2. I do not compete with roles outside my design.
3. I collaborate freely with strengths I do not possess.
4. I accept limitation as part of design, not failure.
5. I align ambition with identity rather than comparison.

Closing Insight: Capacity gaps do not disqualify leaders. Unacknowledged capacity gaps do.

Appendix A.2

Capacity Architecture Diagnostic Tool

(Structural Reinforcement under Load)

This diagnostic is not a personality test. It is an architectural scan. Its purpose is to identify where capacity is present, where strain is emerging, and where reinforcement is required before expansion.

A. Honest Assessment

(Reality Awareness)

1. I understand what I am currently responsible for—formally and practically.

2. I can identify what depends on my presence versus what functions independently.

3. I assess my limits without shame or defensiveness.

4. I distinguish between effort-driven success and structurally supported success.

5. I do not rely on past wins to justify current strain.

Score Insight: Low scores indicate capacity blindness—growth is occurring without accurate self-assessment.

B. Identifying Strain Points

1. Urgency does not escalate into anxiety to (Early Warning Recognition) reactivity.

2. Decision-making does not bottleneck with me unnecessarily.

3. I can step away without systems breaking down.

Dr. Joke Solanke

4. Conflict is processed rather than deferred due to overload.

5. I do not normalize exhaustion as a leadership requirement.

Score Insight: Low scores reveal hidden overload—capacity is being compensated for, not built.

C. Reinforcement before Expansion

(Architectural Reinforcement)

1. I reinforce systems before adding responsibility.

2. I reduce scope when necessary to preserve long-term stability.

3. My boundaries protect sustainability, not just productivity.

4. I redesign workflows when strain appears.

5. I resist expansion when structure is insufficient.

Score Insight: Low scores indicate premature scaling—expansion is outpacing readiness.

D. Structural & Relational Support

(Distributed Load Capacity)

1. Authority and accountability are clearly distributed.

2. Delegation transfers ownership, not just tasks.

3. Outcomes do not depend on constant oversight.

4. I trust systems more than personalities.

5. Collaboration strengthens outcomes rather than slowing them.

Score Insight: Low scores indicate leader-as-bottleneck risk.

E. Review & Sustainability

(Longevity Readiness)

1. I review systems for sustainability, not just performance.

2. I address drift before crisis forces intervention.

3. I can name what would break if responsibility increased today.

4. I adjust rhythm, pace, and load intentionally.

5. I prioritize longevity over speed.

Closing Insight: Growth without reinforcement accelerates failure.

Appendix A.3

Capacity Multiplication & Governance Assessment

(Scale without Collapse)

This diagnostic is not a personality test. It is an architectural scan. Its purpose is to evaluate whether capacity is multiplying through structure and governance—or eroding through centralization and heroics.

A. Delegation as Architecture

(Structural Distribution)

1. Responsibility is distributed, not centralized.
2. Work does not routinely return to me for correction.
3. Decisions are made at appropriate levels.
4. My absence does not stall progress.
5. Delegation is role-based, not personality-based.

Score Insight: Low scores indicate delegation as task assignment rather than capacity preservation.

B. Team Function as Capacity Multipliers

(Collective Load-Bearing)

1. Team members carry distinct domains of ownership.
2. Authority and accountability are aligned.
3. Conflict is processed functionally.

4. The system functions without heroics.

5. Outcomes improve even when I step back.

Score Insight: Teams may exist without being structurally empowered.

C. Collaboration & Network Capacity

(External Load Extension)

1. I collaborate with people who think differently than I do.

2. I seek insight beyond my expertise.

3. I am not threatened by superior competence.

4. I maintain strategic relationships that extend reach.

5. I do not rely on reputation as a substitute for relationship.

Score Insight: Low scores indicate isolation or over-reliance on central authority.

D. Super-Ego / Hero Syndrome Indicators

(Capacity Compensation)

1. I believe it is safer or faster if I handle things myself.

2. I feel pressure to remain indispensable.

3. I struggle to release control even with systems in place.

4. I am praised for holding everything together.

5. I equate relevance with centrality.

Score Insight: High agreement signals capacity compensation—not capacity building. (Higher scores indicate greater risk.)

E. *Governance & Sustainability*

(Protection beyond Presence)

1. Clear principles govern decisions.

2. Standards are enforced consistently.

3. The system protects the mission beyond leadership changes.

4. Accountability exists beyond my oversight.

5. Succession would not destabilize outcomes.

Closing Insight: What is not governed must be carried personally.